New Home Construction Components Manual

RYAN BRAUTOVICH

Copyright © 2013 Ryan Brautovich

All rights reserved. No part of this book may be reproduced or transmitted in any form or by any means, electronic or mechanical, including photocopying, recording, or by any information storage and retrieval system, without the written permission of the Publisher.

Printed in the United States of America

August 2013

ISBN: 978-0-9864404-6-5

"The whole difference between construction and creation is exactly this: that a thing constructed can only be loved after it is constructed; but a thing created is loved before it exists."

~ Charles Dickens

The Construction H.E.L.P. Foundation's Home Construction Audit program makes it easy and painless – through the use of our Home Building System – to understand how to build a home, how to manage your contractor, and how to protect yourself from being taken advantage of and scammed. We demystify the process and remove all of the contractor jargon to give you the building process in easy-to-understand, plain English. The Construction H.E.L.P. Foundation's founder and building expert Ryan Brautovich's exclusive 4-step home building system will ensure you are on the right track – and on budget – every step of the way. For more information about the Construction H.E.L.P Foundation, the Home Construction Audit Program, or any of the educational products, homeowner services, or construction seminars available in your area, please visit **www.HomeConstructionAudit.com**, or **www.ConHelp4U.org**.

TABLE OF CONTENTS
TROUBLESHOOTING GUIDE

PLUMBING

If you notice a leak in a natural gas line…	1
If a water main breaks of a major plumbing leak develops…	1
If you notice a leak under a sink or toilet…	1
If a toilet becomes clogged…	1
If you notice a leak in the tub or shower…	2
If you notice water spots (darkened areas) on your walls or ceilings…	2
If the water temperature is not hot enough…	2

ELECTRICAL

If a complete power outage occurs…	2
If you notice sparks or smelling burning…	3
If there is no power in a bathroom, kitchen or outside receptacle…	3
If there is no power to an electrical outlet…	3
If a luminous light fixture does not work…	3

HEATING AND AIR-CONDITIONING

If the forced air unit (FAU or furnace) is not working properly…	4
If your air-conditioning unit shuts down or will not start (if applicable)…	4
If your air-conditioning unit is continually running (if applicable)…	4
If your air-conditioning unit fails to cool quickly (if applicable.)…	4

MATERIALCHARACTERISTICS AND MAINTENANCE GUIDELINES

APPLIANCES
    MATERIAL CHARACTERISTICS   6
    MAINTENANCE GUIDELINES   7
CABINETS
    MATERIAL CHARACTERISTICS   8
    MAINTENANCE GUIDELINES   9
CONCRETE – DRIVEWAYS, PORCHES, AND SIDEWALKS
    MATERIAL CHARACTERISTICS   9
    MAINTENANCE GUIDELINES   10
CONCRETE – FOUNDATION
    MATERIAL CHARACTERISTICS   10
    MAINTANANCE GUIDELINES   11
COUNTERTOPS – CERAMIC TILE
    MATERIAL CHARACTERISTICS   12
    MAINTENANCE GUIDELINES   13
COUTERTOPS – CULTURED MARBLE
    MATERIAL CHARACTERISTICS   14
    MAINTENANCE GUIDELINES   14
COUNTERTOPS – MANUFACTURED SOLID SURFACE
    MATERIAL CHARACTERISTICS   15
    MATERIAL GUIDELINES   15
COUNTERTOPS – MARBLE AND STONE
    MATERIAL CHARACTERISTICS   15
    MAINTENANCE GUIDELINES   17
DOORS
    MATERIAL CHARACTERISTICS   19
    MAINTENANCE GUIDELINES   19
DOORS – HARDWARE
    MATERIAL CHARACTERISTICS   20
    MAINTENANCE GUIDELINES   20
DOORS – WEATHER-STRIPPING
    MATERIAL CHARACTERISTICS   20
    MAINTENANCE GUIDELINES   21
DRYWALL
    MATERIAL CHARACTERISTICS   21
    MAINTENANCE GUIDELINES   22

ELECTRICAL	
MATERIAL CHARACTERISTICS	22
MAINTENANCE GUIDELINES	23
FANS – CEILING	
MATERIAL CHARACTERISTICS	24
MAINTENANCE GUIDELINES	24
FENCES/GATES – WOOD	
MATERIAL CHARACTERISTICS	24
MAINTENANCE GUIDELINES	25
FENCES – MASONRY WALLS	
MATERIAL CHARACTERISTICS	26
MAINTENANCE GUIDELINES	27
FENCES – METAL	
MATERIAL CHARACTERISTICS	27
MAINTENANCE GUIDELINES	28
FIREPLACE – DIRECT VENT & WOOD BURNING	
MATERIAL CHARACTERISTICS	29
MAINTENANCE GUIDELINES	30
FLOORING – GENERAL	
MATERIAL CHARACTERISTICS	30
MATERIAL GUIDELINES	31
FLOORING – CARPET	
MATERIAL CHARACTERISTICS	32
MAINTENANCE GUIDELINES	32
FLOORING – CERAMIC TILE	
MAINTENANCE GUIDELINES	34
FLOORING – MARBLE AND STONE	
MATERIAL CHARACTERISTICS	36
MAINTENANCE GUIDELINES	37
FLOORING – VINYL	
MATERIAL CHARACTERISTICS	39
MAINTENANCE GUIDELINES	39
FLOORING – WOOD	
MATERIAL CHARACTERISTICS	40
MAINTENANCE GUIDELINES	41
FOOD DISPOSAL	
MATERIAL CHARACTERISTICS	42
MAINTENANCE GUIDELINES	42
OPERATING GUIDELINES	43

FRAMING
    MATERIAL CHARACTERISTICS — 44
        Walls — 44
        Roof Trusses/Attic — 44
        Second Story Floors — 44
    MAINTENANCE GUIDELINES — 45
GARAGE DOORS (SECTIONAL ROLL-UP)
    MATERIAL CHARACTERISTICS — 45
    MAINTENANCE GUIDELINES — 46
GAS METER
    MATERIAL CHARACTERISTICS — 47
    MAINTENANCE GUIDELINES — 47
HVAC – AIR CONDITIONING
    MATERIAL CHARACTERISTICS — 47
    MAINTENANCE GUIDELINES — 48
    OPERATING GUIDELINES — 48
    TROUBLESHOOTING — 49
    CONDENSATION — 49
HVAC – HEATING
    MATERIAL CHARACTERISTICS — 50
    MAINTENANCE GUIDELINES — 51
    OPERATING GUIDELINES — 52
    TROUBLESHOOTING — 52
LANDSCAPE AND IRRIGATION
    MAINTENANCE GUIDELINES — 52
PAINTED SURFACES – EXTERIOR
    MATERIAL CHARACTERISTICS — 55
    MAINTENANCE GUIDELINES — 55
PAINTED SURFACES – INTERIOR
    MATERIAL CHARACTERISTICS — 56
    MAINTENANCE GUIDELINES — 57
PEST CONTROL
    MATERIAL CHARACTERISTICS — 58
PLUMBING – FAUCETS
    MATERIAL CHARACTERISTICS — 58
    MAINTENANCE GUIDELINES — 59
PLUMBING – HOT WATER HEATER
    MATERIAL CHARACTERISTICS — 59
    MAINTENANCE GUIDELINES — 60
    OPERATION GUIDELINES — 60

PLUMBING – PORCELAIN FIXUTRES
    MATERIAL CHARACTERISTICS   61
    MAINTENANCE GUIDELINES   61
PLUMBING – TUB & SHOWER
    MATERIAL CHARACTERISTICS   62
    MAINTENANCE GUIDELINES   62
PLUMBING – WASTE LINES
    MATERIAL CHARACTERISTICS   63
    MAINTENANCE GUIDELINES   64
PLUMBING – WATER SYSTEM
    MATERIAL CHARACTERISTICS   65
    MAINTENANCE GUIDELINES   67
ROOF AND GUTTERS
    MATERIAL CHARACTERISTICS   67
    MAINTENANCE GUIDELINES   68
SHOWER ENCLOSURE
    MATERIAL CHARACTERISTICS   69
    MAINTENANCE GUIDELINES   69
SHOWER WALLS – CERAMIC TILE
    MATERIAL CHARACTERISTICS   70
    MAINTENANCE GUIDELINES   70
SMOKE DETECTORS
    MATERIAL CHARACTERISTICS   70
    MAINTENANCE GUIDELINES   71
STUCCO
    MATERIAL CHARACTERISTICS   73
    MAINTENANCE GUIDELINES   74
VENEER – MASONRY
    MATERIAL CHARACTERISTICS   74
    MAINTENANCE GUIDELINES   75
VENTS
    MATERIAL CHARACTERISTICS   75
    MAINTENANCE GUIDELINES   75
WINDOWS, SLIDING DOORS AND SCREENS
    MATERIAL CHARACTERISTICS   76
    MAINTENANCE GUIDELINES   78
YARD DRAINAGE
    MATERIAL CHARACTERISTICS   79
    MAINTENANCE GUIDELINES   79
    DESIGN GUIDELINES   80

TROUBLE SHOOTING GUIDE

PLUMBING

If you notice a leak in a natural gas line…

For your protection, The Gas Company adds a distinctive odor to natural gas, so leaks are easily detected. If you smell a natural gas odor in your home, have everyone go outside. Do not turn on or off anything electrical, including lights, appliances or tools. Turn off the gas at the gas meter. Do not use any phones in your house; use your neighbor's telephone or a cellular phone from outside your home to call your local Gas provider to report the leakage. Do not light matches, candles, cigarettes, etc. Call the Fire Department immediately if you can't reach your local Gas provider.

If a water main breaks of a major plumbing leak develops…

Turn off the main water valve to your house. The location of the main water valve should have been pointed out during your New Home Orientation. The water meter and main valve are generally located in a concrete meter box in the ground in the vicinity of where the water line enters the property; typically at the front of the house near the street. Additionally, there is sometimes a water valve where the water enters the house, typically found in the vicinity of where the gas, electric utilities also enter the house (This valve will shut off water to the house. Outdoor water, i.e. irrigation will remain on). It is important the members of you household know the location of this valve and how to operate it. Ask the Customer Service Office for a demonstration of the use of the valve shutoff if needed.

If you notice a leak under a sink or toilet…

Turn off the water to the fixture by using the shutoff valves located under or behind the unit. The locations of the water shutoffs should have been pointed out during your New Home Orientation. Arrange for service.

If a toilet becomes clogged…

Turn off the water to the fixture. Use a household plunger to try to clear the line. If not successful, arrange for service.

If you notice a leak in the tub or shower…

Turn off the water to the fixture and arrange for service. Do not use the shower or tub until service can be provided.

If you notice water spots (darkened areas) on your walls or ceilings…

You may have a water leak. Determine the source of water if possible and take steps to prevent further damage. If the leak can be traced to one location (one toilet, sink or tub), turn off the water to the fixture. Contact your Builder's Customer Service Department for assistance. If the leak cannot be isolated, turn off the main water service to the house. Call your Builder's Customer Service Department to report a plumbing emergency.

If the water temperature is not hot enough…

Adjust the temperature at the water heater by following the Manufacturers' instructions printed on the tank. **CAUTION!** Before entering the tub or shower, always turn on water and adjust it to a safe and proper temperature. Children, elderly people (or any person), should never be placed in a tub or shower before the water is turned on and the temperature safely adjusted in order to avoid accidental burns.

ELECTRICAL

If a complete power outage occurs…

See if your neighbors have electrical power. If the power is off throughout your neighborhood, call your electricity provider to report the outage. If the outage is limited to your home, follow the next steps.

Inspect all circuit breakers, including the main breaker. If a breaker appears damaged leave it off and call the electrical contractor who installed the system, as well your Builder's Customer Service Department.

If the breakers do not appear to be damaged, turn them all off and back on again, one at a time. If power does not resume, call the electrical contractor who installed the system, as well your Builder's Customer Service Department.

IMPORTANT NOTE: If your main circuit breaker trips or is turned off, wait 2-3 minutes before turning it on. Then, restore power to the other circuits one by one. This avoids overloading the system.

If you notice sparks or smelling burning...

Find the location of the odor or sparks. If an appliance is plugged into the outlet, check the appliance for a short in the cord or other problem and unplug it. If this is not the problem, shut off the problem circuit and call the electrical contractor who installed the system, as well your Builder's Customer Service Department.

IMPORTANT NOTE: Immediately call the fire department at 911 if there is any possibility of a fire.

If there is no power in a bathroom, kitchen or outside receptacle...

These receptacles may be connected to a Ground Fault Circuit Interrupt (GFCI) device designed to interrupt the flow of electricity preventing electrical injury or damage. Locate the nearest GFCI outlet. If the test button has tripped, press the reset button to restore power. If power is not restored, determine if the circuit is being overloaded. Two hair dryers or other appliances being used on one circuit could cause the breaker to trip.

IMPORTANT NOTE: Avoid the use of power tools and appliances, especially refrigerators and freezers, in GFI outlets.

If there is no power to an electrical outlet...

Make sure a wall switch which may be turned off does not control the outlet (otherwise known as a half hot outlet). Once this is determined, inspect the circuit breakers and reset any which are in the OFF position.

If a luminous light fixture does not work...

Make sure all fluorescent bulbs are installed properly. Adjust any tubes which are flickering or buzzing. Check wall switches and circuit breakers.

HEATING AND AIR-CONDITIONING (WHERE APPLICABLE)

If the forced air unit (FAU or furnace) is not working properly...

Make sure the thermostat is set to a temperature higher than the room air and the unit has power and the interlock switch is closed. Determine the safety access door is closed properly. Make sure the circuit breaker is in the ON position and the gas service is ON. Check the fuse on the unit and replace if necessary. Finally, check to see the gas valve is in the ON position and the pilot light or intermittent sparking device is working. If you are unable to isolate the problem, call the heating and air-conditioning subcontractor for service.

If your air-conditioning unit shuts down or will not start (if applicable)...

Make sure the thermostat is set to a temperature which is cooler than the room air. Then, turn the air conditioner OFF at the thermostat and inspect the circuit breaker. If the breaker is tripped reset it and restore power to the unit. If it does not restart, check the air conditioner fuse to make sure it is usable and properly installed. This fuse is in the outside fuse box located near the compressor unit.

If your air-conditioning unit is continually running (if applicable)...

Set your thermostat to no more than 20 degrees below peak outside air temperature. On particularly hot days, it may run continually. It is important you change the filters in your unit regularly.

If your air-conditioning unit fails to cool quickly (if applicable.)...

Your air conditioner must be on constantly during warm months because it is not designed to cool your home quickly. Choose a comfortable setting for your thermostat and give the unit ample time to reach the desired temperature. In very warm weather this may take longer.

MATERIAL CHARACTERISTICS AND MAINTENANCE GUIDELINES

All construction materials, appliances and equipment have projected life expectancy maximums and performance thresholds. The intensity of use and the timeliness and effectiveness of preventive maintenance directly affect all components. To help prolong the enjoyment and longevity of your new home, we offer these **MATERIAL CHARACTERISTICS AND MAINTENANCE GUIDELINES** as an effort to provide helpful maintenance information. In case of a contradiction in these guidelines, refer to the manufacturers' instructions and recommendations which take precedence, or contact the Customer Service Office for further assistance.

These suggestions and guidelines are not all inclusive and you should remember the performance of the systems and materials will vary with each individual home. If a component in your home is not performing to your expectations after following the prescribed maintenance, please bring the situation to the attention of your Builder's Customer Service Office for informational assistance or for directions in submitting a **Warranty Service Request,** if appropriate.

APPLIANCES

MATERIAL CHARACTERISTICS

Appliances are considered "consumer products" and are specifically covered by a Manufacturers' warranty. To activate your warranty and service, be sure to complete and mail in the warranty registration cards right after you move in.

Home appliances, such as your range, microwave and dishwasher come with an explanation of features, care and cleaning requirements and directions on how to obtain warranty service.

Your dishwasher will be installed with a water supply hookup. Should the dishwasher malfunction and cause a water leak, the water shutoff valve is located in the cabinet beneath the kitchen sink. It is possible the same supply valve used for the dishwasher controls the cold water supply for the kitchen sink.

Although water supply valves have been installed in the home for a refrigerator icemaker and washing machine, the Homeowner is responsible for the connection of the appliance(s) to the supply valve(s). After the connection has been made, turn the shutoff valve counter-clockwise to turn the water ON. These shutoff valves will be demonstrated to you during your New Home Orientation. These valves are similar to the sink faucet valves.

The common rubber hoses on your washing machine tend to wear out over time, similar to a radiator hose on a car. A burst hose can cause a tremendous amount of water damage to the home, especially if the home happens to be unoccupied when the event occurs. It is advisable to invest in upgraded hoses with braided stainless steel jacketing (these types of hoses are also available for the icemaker connection). Regardless, consult with a plumber or your home improvements center as to the anticipated life span of your hose(s) and then replace them on the timetable even if they do not show signs of wearing out.

If a gas appliance has been installed in your home, the in-line shutoff valve will be demonstrated to you. If the appliance is leaking gas, turn the valve perpendicular to the line to the "OFF" position and ventilate the room. Follow the instructions in the **TROUBLESHOOTING GUIDE** for contacting your local Gas provider. If you still smell a gas odor after turning OFF the in-line valve and ventilating the room, turn OFF the main supply to the house at the gas meter and call the gas company.

If a gas stub has been provided for supply to a clothes dryer. <u>Please note a shutoff valve has not been supplied or installed for connection to the clothes dryer.</u> The Homeowner is responsible for the connection of the appliance to the supply. An in-line shutoff should be installed directly onto the gas stub. The gas flex line can then be run from the shutoff to the appliance. Consult with your local Gas provider regarding the proper installation procedure.

MAINTENANCE GUIDELINES

1. Thoroughly read the owner's manual(s) supplied with your appliance(s). Although much of the information may seem like common sense, some points may differ significantly from previous products you have owned or operated. Always follow the operation and safety guidelines and requirements contained in the publication.

2. It is the homeowners' responsibility to see that the flex vent on their dryer is properly attached to the fixed vent provided in their home. It is recommended that this hook-up be done by a qualified appliance installer or plumber. Once installed, the homeowners should check the vent system regularly, both at the dryer unit and where the vent exits the home, to be certain that airflow is unobstructed and the vent is free of lint build-up.
3. Power assist fans to the dryer venting system are required by the building code in some plan types. If a dryer assist fan was installed in your new home, this unit will require periodic maintenance by a professional (heating and air contractor or electrician).
4. Never put lye or drain clearing chemicals into the dishwasher as they may cause permanent damage.
5. Do not use steel wool, abrasives, ammonia or commercial oven cleaners on metal parts of your appliances. To safely clean these surfaces, wash with a mild soap, rinse, and then dry with a soft cloth. Follow Manufacturer's cleaning recommendations.
6. Glass cleaner may be used for glass surfaces, and polish with a soft, dry cloth. Do not allow the water or cleaner to run down inside openings in the glass.

CABINETS

MATERIAL CHARACTERISTICS

The cabinetry in your home has a factory-applied finish. Only high quality hardwoods are used for the fabrication of the cabinets. Because no two trees are alike, the lumber cut from the trees varies in color and in character markings, such as grain patterns and mineral marks. Some species of wood will even vary in color depending on the time of year it is harvested.

You may notice some variations in the appearance of your cabinets due to natural imperfections in the wood and inconsistencies in the wood grain. Variations in wood grain and color on stained wood cabinets doors, drawers, end panels, corn mold, filler panels and wood trim are inherent to natural wood surface which create the warmth and natural beauty of the finished product. The variations are normal and unavoidable, and are not considered defects.

If your cabinets have a stain finish, the stain is sealed at the factory with a clear acrylic coating. The finish may tend to turn yellow due to exposure to sunlight and/or heat generated by appliances in the kitchen. Also, as the cabinet's age, the hardwood may start to darken. Because of these normal material characteristics, any replacement parts cannot be guaranteed to match the existing cabinets.

Please note the stain on pre-finished cabinets might not match the stain on pre-finished wood floor, entry doors, stair rails, stair tread nosing, etc.

MAINTENANCE GUIDELINES

1. Clean and polish your wood cabinets as you do your fine wood furniture. For a cleaning solution use a mild solution of dishwashing soap and water. Dry completely and do not allow water or other liquids to remain on the surface. Apply furniture wax or oil for surface protection.
2. To clean painted, laminated or thermofoil surfaces, use only a mild soap with warm water. Do not use any cleaning product which contains an abrasive of any kind. Consult professional refinisher for scratches and/or gouges.
3. **Note:** If repairs or replacements are scheduled, please do not clean or polish the affected surfaces until the defects are corrected.

CONCRETE – DRIVEWAYS, PORCHES, AND SIDEWALKS

MATERIAL CHARACTERISTICS

Concrete expands with summer heat and contracts with winter cold. Though the greatest care was taken in its installation, the very nature of concrete makes it impossible to prevent some minor cracking and/or staining, which is therefore considered normal. Though some cracking is normal, areas installed by the original builder with significant vertical displacement or cracks that are excessive may need to be evaluated. (For further information refer to Construction Performance Guidelines). Minor cracking will not negatively affect the integrity of the installation.

While the concrete is going through the curing process, moisture is evaporating through the surface and may cause discoloration. This characteristic can also be dependent upon the weather at the time the concrete was poured, as well as upon the moisture content of the concrete installed which will vary from batch to batch. Concrete can take years to completely cure at which time the color may become somewhat uniform in appearance.

Because of these material characteristics, if portions of the concrete driveways, porches or walkways must be removed and placed under warranty, color match cannot be guaranteed. Only the portion of concrete to be removed due to defect will be replaced, and the entire installation will never be removed or replaced only to facilitate color matching. Driveways will typically be replaced in sectional increments of ¼, 1/3, ½ (or complete) depending on damage and the location of existing expansion joints. Sidewalk will typically be replaced from expansion joint to expansion joint.

Concrete driveways are designed to withstand the weight of common private passenger vehicles. In order to avoid cracking, do not allow heavy equipment such as moving vans, concrete trucks, tractors, dump trucks, delivery trucks, etc., to drive on the driveway.

If the Homeowner chooses to install additional concrete areas after occupancy, be certain the finished surface does not cover the weep screed (review the section on Stucco). Also if planting strips are created by the addition of the concrete, it is important to add area drains so runoff water has an escape outlet. When the concrete is poured, a felt expansion joint should be used between the concrete and the house foundation. The finished surface of the concrete should also slope away from the home so as to prevent runoff water from entering the interior of the home.

MAINTENANCE GUIDELINES

1. Concrete surfaces should be protected from potted plants. The pot should be elevated to allow air circulation underneath, or moved periodically to prevent water from collecting underneath and staining the concrete.
2. Pay attention to the location and type of doormat you use, as all doormats can cause staining to concrete if prolonged moisture is allowed to collect underneath.
3. If spills or stains occur, special cleaners are commonly available for cleaning concrete, including stains from grease and oil.

CONCRETE – FOUNDATION

MATERIAL CHARACTERISTICS

The structural slab of your home has been designed with consideration of the weight and design of the building, wind exposure, seismic conditions and soil expansion potential. **Any modification of the slab, such as drilling holes, grinding the surface down or otherwise interfering with its structural integrity, or the overstressing of the slab by placing objects heavier than the slab is designed to carry, can result in slab failure.** Though the greatest care was taken in its installation, the very nature of concrete makes it impossible to prevent some minor cracking. This will not affect your home's structural integrity.

The structural slab of your home may have been constructed with a post-tensioning process utilizing stretched steel cables, crisscrossed within the slabs with allow the foundation to flex without excessive cracking. **Warning: The post-tension steel cables are under pressure. Concrete modification should not commence without first de-tensioning the cables. Cutting or slicing the tensioned cables can cause serious injury as well as severe damage to the slab and/or structure.** If modifying the slab for remodeling purposes use only a contractor in possession of a current concrete license issued by the appropriate State governing agency, to perform the work.

Regardless of the type of slab used to construct your home (conventional or post tension), any modification of the slab will automatically void the warranty.

Garage floors are provided as a functional place to park your car and are not intended or designed to be aesthetically pleasing. At time of delivery of the home, the garage floor will have been cleaned. Some stains, discoloration, minor cracks and slight gouges or chips may be visible but are NOT considered defects.

MAINTANANCE GUIDELINES

1. If spills or stains occur, special cleaners are commonly available for cleaning grease and oil from concrete garage floors.
2. It is highly recommended you do not store any boxes directly on the garage floor. Moisture from the concrete is evaporating during the curing process and can cause mildew or other moisture damage to non-waterproof items left in direct contact with the concrete.

COUNTERTOPS – CERAMIC TILE

MATERIAL CHARACTERISTICS

Ceramic tile is a fired or baked clay product with a hard and brittle glaze applied to the surface for color and/or texture. The manufacture of tile even in modern times remains more of an art than a science. Therefore, even if tile is manufactured to the strict tolerances the individual pieces will have some inherent flaws. Slight color variations from tile to tile will be typical in genuine glazed ceramic tiles. Also, due to the firing process there may be a slight surface variation, or it may not be perfectly flat. Ceramic tiles with a surface texture will, of course, vary in height.

Ceramic tile liners of specialty apron tiles are typically not manufactured by the same source as the field tile and therefore will vary from the field tile. Variation in size and or color within individual liners or within the shipment of liners may result in the appearance of unevenness in the finished product.

Variable job site conditions, variations and irregularities of the tile or stone will require decisions on layout, installation techniques and grout joint widths. The installers will make these decisions at the time of installation and at their sole discretion. In the event there is a different method of installation available, as determined by a third party, it will not render the original installation to be considered defective.

Grouting the joints between tiles will complete the installation of the ceramic tile countertop. There are two common types of grout joint installations. If the tiles are butted together to create a separation of not more than 1/8 inch in width, then an unsanded polyblend grout is used. If the joint between the tiles is set at 1/8 inch in width, then an unsanded polyblend grout is used. If the joint between the tiles is set at 1/8 inch to 1/2 inch in width, the grouting is done with a sanded polyblend grout. Colored grouts for either application may vary in shade from the sample used to select the color due to the wide variety of tiles available, environmental conditions and finishing techniques. The elements of nature, including but not limited to sun, temperature, food or chemical reactions, may combine with aging process to change the color of the grout in varying degrees over time.

Certain areas of colored grout on any given countertop area may also vary in color. If repair or replacement of tile or grout areas is required, matching the original or changed color of the remaining color tile grout may be impossible. Colored grout can also cause the discoloration, flecking and/or cracked appearance of the ceramic tile in the areas where colored grout is used. If grout is replaced, there is no guarantee that the replacement color will match that of the original installation.

Efflorescence (a whitish powder) can appear on the joints or along the edges of the tiles. This is a chemical reaction of soluble salts and water, common to all cement products. This material is harmless and can be removed by using a stiff bristle brush with clean water. It may take some time before it will completely disappear through normal use.

Separations and cracks in the grout between the tiles and between those tiles and backsplashes, bathtubs, shower pans, etc. are normal and are not covered by the warranty. Repair of cracked grout is considered a Homeowner maintenance item. The cracks can be repaired with a prepared and pre-mixed grout purchased from a paint or hardware store.

Settlement of the house and/or expansion or contraction of the tile substrate may also cause hairline cracks in ceramic tile or grout. This is considered normal and these tiles and/or grout cracks are not covered under warranty.

MAINTENANCE GUIDELINES

1. All ceramic tile surfaces installed in your new home are unsealed. The application of a sealer specifically formulated for use with this particular material, as recommended by the manufacturer, is highly advisable. There are several products available with varying Material Characteristics. Follow product instructions for application and maintenance. It is advisable to test an area which is not visible to make sure you are satisfied with the product and the results
2. Ceramic tile may be cleaned daily with a damp cloth or mop. Extremely dirty areas may be cleaned with a "natural" cleaner and water. Do not use any type of cleansers which contain chemicals or abrasives. Do not use steel wool, acids, or metallic brushes on the tile or grout as damage may result.
3. No waxing or polishing of ceramic tile is needed. You may use one-half teaspoon full of lemon oil sprinkled on soft cloth to remove hard water spots and restore shine to your new tile. Do not do this more frequently than one (1) time per month.
4. Always clean up liquid spills and water accumulations as soon as detected, to avoid staining and penetration of moisture through the

grout. If the grout becomes stained, use a mild/diluted bleaching solution or a pre-mixed product, such as Soft Scrub with Bleach. Always rinse thoroughly and wipe with a soft cloth, being careful not to let the bleach solution drip or accumulate onto any adjacent surfaces, which could cause further damage. For colored grouts, color stains and paints are available from ceramic tile stores which can give your grout surface a like-new appearance.

5. To repair cracked grout between tiles, obtain the proper type and color of grout from a home improvement center. The grout may be available pre-mixed. In either case, follow the manufacturer's instructions for use. After the replacement of the grout, wash the area several times with warm water and a sponge to remove the haze residue left behind by the grout. Do not use harsh cleaning agents, steel wool pads, etc., which can scratch or damage the surface of your tile. Do not wash excess grout down the drain, which could cause blockage and cause the need for plumbing repairs.

6. For repair of cracked grout joints at tiled tubs or shower pans, it is typical to fill this joint with a silicone-based caulk available from your home improvement store. There may be repeated movement between the ceramic tile and tub or shower pan due to shrinkage in the framing materials, and a silicone based caulk will maintain flexibility and be less prone to further cracking. When caulk is applied in these locations, it will need to be redone from time to time.

COUTERTOPS – CULTURED MARBLE

MATERIAL CHARACTERISTICS

To avoid staining of cultured marble surfaces, do not allow spilled personal care products (cosmetics, perfumes, locations, etc.) to remain on the counter.

MAINTENANCE GUIDELINES

1. Clean the cultured marble surface periodically with mild soap and water. Never use abrasive cleaners and/or scouring pads.
2. Automobile wax can be applied as water repellent and to provide a shine, or as recommended by the manufacturer.

COUNTERTOPS – MANUFACTURED SOLID SURFACE

MATERIAL CHARACTERISTICS

You may have selected a manufactured solid surface material such as "DuPont Corian" for countertop installation in your home. Special care is required to keep your manufactured solid surface countertops in "as new" condition. Please refer to the Manufacturer's recommendations for care and maintenance guidelines.

The darker jewel tone and/or designer colors used on solid surface counters are higher maintenance than the lighter, translucent colors which are recommended for normal and high usage work surfaces. The darker colors will show dust, marks and scratches from normal use, more so than the lighter colors. The darker colors are meant to be used as accent materials rather than for use as the main work surface, and are therefore not recommended in instances where higher maintenance will be a concern.

MATERIAL GUIDELINES

1. See Manufacturer's guidelines for instructions on the maintenance of your specific product.

COUNTERTOPS – MARBLE AND STONE

MATERIAL CHARACTERISTICS

Marble/natural stone is a product of nature exhibiting unique color and texture variations in each piece, and no two pieces will be exactly the same. Variations of color, shading, veining, texture, pattern, thickness and marbling, as well as natural imperfections (such as pitting, scaling, fissures or factory filler) are all considered normal. No guarantees are made that the sample presented to the homebuyer for selection will match the actual material to be installed; the display sample will only exhibit the average color, texture, shading and marking of the natural stone.

If selecting a marble or stone tile (as opposed to a slab installation) for a countertop, please be aware the tiles cannot match slab material and vise versa. Stone moldings will also not match stone tiles or slab exactly and are subject to the same shading, texture, veining and other natural variances. Because of imperfect quarrying methods the overall dimension of the pieces may not be exact, which will cause variation in the grout lines. Variation in thickness of the pieces will cause height differences between the tiles which is considered normal.

Slab granite is a heavy natural stone material quarried from earth. No two slabs are alike. Each slab will have inherent variations; color, shading veining, pitting, fissures and textures. No two pieces of stone will ever look exactly the same even when cut from the same block of material. The natural products installed in your home will look different from the showroom samples and model installations.

Granite and natural stone products may crack from time to time for reasons that are not due to mishandling or poor installation. In any event, when a portion of slab requires replacement whether through fault of installation or not, the method of fixing the damage will be at the Builder's discretion. The Builder will endeavor to match the existing material as closely as possible, and a perfect match is never possible. The area of replacement may be limited to the area of the damage, either creating a new seam where the damaged material is replaced or replacing the material to the nearest seam. The Builder will attempt to match any materials that are replaced as closely as possible. Do not sit on countertops or place heavy tools upon them that may cause stress and cracks in the surface.

Marble/natural stones are considered very durable, and require maintenance. Periodic upkeep is recommended. Most stones are porous and readily absorb liquids and moisture, and will stain from any topical spill. All acids, including those found in many foods, fruits and beverages will likely etch the surface of polished stone, even if the stone has been sealed. Green marbled stone is especially susceptible to etching. In bath areas stone surfaces can also be susceptible to discoloration from soap, makeup products and hairsprays.

Variable job site conditions, variations and irregularities of the tile or stone require decisions on layout, installation techniques and grout joint widths. The installers will make these decisions at the time of installation.

Grouting the joints between tiles will complete the installation of the marble or stone tile countertop. There are two common types of grout joint installations. If the tiles are butted together to create a separation of not more than 1/8 inch in width, then an un-sanded polyblend grout is used. If the joint between the tiles is set at 1/8 inch to 1/2 inch in width, the grouting is done with a sanded polyblend grout.

Colored grouts for either application may vary in shade from the sample used to select the color due to the wide variety of tiles available, environmental conditions and finishing techniques. Light to mid-tone grout colors generally exhibits a tendency toward a wider shade variation than do dark colors. The elements of nature, including but not limited to sun, temperature, food or chemical reactions, may combine with aging process to change the color of the grout in varying degrees over time.

Certain areas of colored grout on any given countertop area may also vary in color. If repair or replacement of tile or grout areas is required, matching the original or changed color of the remaining colored grout may be impossible. Colored grout can also cause the discoloration, flecking and/or cracked appearance of the marble or stone tile in the areas where colored grout is used.

Use of colored grout with a stone surface may cause discoloration of the marble/natural stone due to the porosity of the material. The colored grout may also accentuate normal irregularities of the marble/stone.

Efflorescence (a whitish powder) can appear on the joints or along the edges of the tile. This is a chemical reaction of soluble salts and water, common to all cement products. This material is harmless and can be removed by using a stiff bristle brush with clean water. It may take some time before it will completely disappear through normal use.

Separations and cracks in the grout between the tiles and between those tiles and backsplashes, bathtubs, shower pants, etc. are normal. Repair of cracked grout is a Homeowner maintenance item. The cracks can be repaired with a pre-mixed grout purchased from a paint or hardware store.

Settlement of the house and/or expansion or contraction of the tile substrate may also cause hairline cracks in ceramic tile or grout. This is considered normal.

MAINTENANCE GUIDELINES

1. All marble/natural stone floor surfaces installed in your new home are unsealed. The application of a sealer specifically formulated for use with this particular material as recommended by the manufacturer is highly advisable. The sealer should be one which allows the stone to "breathe." There are several products available with varying material characteristics. Follow product instructions for application and maintenance. It is advisable to test an area

which is not visible to make sure you are satisfied with the product and the results. Do not apply a grout sealer for a minimum of two (2) weeks after the date of installation.
2. Periodic cleaning of all stone surfaces with warm water is recommended to remove ordinary dirty and dust build up.
3. For more intensive cleaning, consult with the manufacturer of the stone for the type of cleaning product you should use specific to your stone.
4. Avoid the use of cleaning products which have distinctive colors, this includes oil based dressing or colored waxes. Over time, these tend to impart their character into the stone.
5. Avoid cleansers which contain grit or are highly alkaline in composition. Especially avoid mop and shine products typically obtained off of the grocer's shelf, as the alkaline will penetrate the surface of the material and then form crystals in the stone. The pressure exerted by the crystals will pop the stone leaking pits and gouges in the surface.
6. Always clean up liquid spill and water accumulations as soon as detected, to avoid staining and penetration of moisture through the grout into the substructure.
7. If the grouting becomes stained, use a mild bleaching solution (diluted to 1 part bleach to 4 parts water). Simply apply a small amount of this mixture and scrub with a soft bristly brush. Avoid contact of this mixture on the stone.
8. Colored grouts, color stains and paints are available from ceramic tiles stores which can give your grout surface a new appearance. Remember the colored stain may leach into the porous stone.
9. To repair cracked grout between tiles, obtain the proper type and color of grout from a home improvement center. The grout may be available pre-mixed. In either case, follow the manufacturer's instructions for use. After the replacement of the grout, wash the area several times with warm water and a sponge to remove the haze residue left behind by the grout. Do not use harsh cleaning agents, steel wood pads, etc., which can scratch or damage the surface of your tile. Be careful not to wash excess grout down the drain, which could cause blockage and cause the need for repairs.
10. For repair of cracked grout joints at tiled tubs or shower pans, it may be more effective to fill this joint with a silicone-based caulk available from your local home improvement store. There may be repeated movement between the ceramic tile and tub or shower pan due to shrinkage in the framing materials, and a silicone based caulk will maintain flexibility and be less prone to further cracking. A re-application of the caulk may be necessary from time to time.

DOORS

MATERIAL CHARACTERISTICS

All interior passage and closet doors, exterior French doors, service, garage and home entry doors have been installed to meet or exceed National Woodwork Manufacturers Association Standards, and are protected with either a stain or a paint finish.

The climate conditions and the normal drying of the wood creates shrinkage, expansion and contraction, which often causes warping, twisting, cracking, or causes joints to open, all of which is beyond the control of the Builder. These occurrences are therefore not considered defects, unless they exceed allowable tolerances (SEE CONSTRUCTION PERFORMANCE GUIDELINES).

The space between the flooring and the bottom of the door is provided for air circulation when the door is closed. If you modify the flooring in the future please be advised the door may need to be trimmed in order to close properly and provide air circulation over the new flooring surface. If you trim the bottom of the door the fresh cut should be sealed with a stain or primer coat of paint.

MAINTENANCE GUIDELINES

1. Painted doors require regular maintenance. Prevent deterioration of your exterior doors by regularly repainting them with quality exterior enamel paint and be sure to use the same type of exterior enamel paint (latex, etc.) which you are painting over.
2. Gloss paints and certain colors of paint are difficult to touch-up evenly so you may need to consider painting the entire door rather than just touching-up certain areas.
3. Keep all edges, including the bottom edge of both interior and exterior doors, painted (sealed) to prevent moisture from penetrating the doors and causing de-lamination and/or warping.
4. If a door sticks due to change in weather (dry to wet climate), do not plane the door. Coat the surface which sticks with bar soap. As the door dries out (cures), it should operate normally.
5. Door panel inserts are designed to shrink and expand with varying weather and/or temperature conditions and an unpainted surface may be exposed when this occurs. This is normal and is designed to prevent both panel and joint cracking. Paint touch-up is a Homeowner maintenance item and you paint the exposed surface(s) as they occur.

DOORS – HARDWARE

MATERIAL CHARACTERISTICS

Door hardware exposed to the elements is coated with a clear protective sealer, which will keep the hardware looking new as long as the coating integrity remains intact. Oils from the hand, humidity, salt and rain, and exposure to extreme sunlight will cause the hardware to lose its brilliance. Scratches from keys or abrasives in cleaners will likely cause the protective sealer to break down, causing discoloration of the exposed metal or peeling of the clear coat.

MAINTENANCE GUIDELINES

1. Lubricate the lock assembly according to Manufacturer's directions once every six (6) months, or as needed (most manufacturers recommend lubricating with dry graphite). Be careful not to spill any lubricant on the hardware finish.
2. To clean, simply use a soft, clean, dry cloth. Do not use any type of chemical or abrasive cleaning solution.
3. Detergents, alcohol, varnishes, paint remover, thinners and any similar chemicals should not be applied to or be used in the vicinity of the hardware surface, as these will damage the finish.
4. Sharp objects like knives, door keys, clothes hangers and rings can scratch the protective coating and initiate corrosion.
5. Over time, and depending on usage of the door hardware, the protective coating may wear away. If the protective coating is not replaced, the hardware may begin to corrode. Contact the manufacturer for re-coating procedures.

DOORS – WEATHER-STRIPPING

MATERIAL CHARACTERISTICS

Door weather-strip is installed at the threshold and the doorjamb of exterior doors to seal off the closed door against wind, water and weather. Weather-stripping as the side and top of doorjambs is integral with a heavy-duty compression strip. This strip will fill the void between the door surface and the doorjamb when the door is closed.

The door threshold is sloped away from the door so any water which hits the door will roll off and away from the house. The metal and vinyl strip at the bottom of the door is the door shoe and works to seal the gap between the bottom of the door and the threshold. The door shoe is adjustable and needs to be inspected by the Homeowner and adjusted to eliminate gaps as the house settles.

It is normal there may be some slight air moisture infiltration, especially during heavy storms with high winds and/or driving rain. If this becomes problematic the Homeowner may adjust the door lock(s) to latch the door(s) tighter and improve the seal.

When washing down the porch or patio in front of the door, do not spray the door or weather-stripping directly with a garden hose, as it is possible direct water pressure against the door will cause the door to leak. Also, make certain that irrigation sprinklers do not direct water against the door and/or weather-stripping.

When moving into the home, to avoid scratches or denting, the door thresholds should be protected from heavy furniture or moving equipment. If scratches occur they can be touched up careful by the Homeowner using a paint product purchased at any home improvement or paint store.

MAINTENANCE GUIDELINES

1. Inspect weather-stripping to door contact every six (6) months to check for the proper seal. Inspect and adjust the door sweep as necessary.
2. To clean, simply use a soft, clean, dry cloth. Do not use any type of chemical or abrasive cleaning solution.
3. Detergents, alcohol, varnishes, paint remover, thinners and any similar chemicals should not be applied to or used in the vicinity of the threshold or door shoe surface, as these will damage the finish. Over time, and depending on usage of the door, the factory finish on the threshold may wear away. Products are available which may be applied to touch up scratches and normal wear and tear.

DRYWALL

MATERIAL CHARACTERISTICS

Drywall is a standard construction product and is applied to most of the internal wall surfaces of your home. The drywall is applied in sheets, with the vertical joints staggered to help mask the appearance of the joints in the final fixture. The installation process cannot completely conceal the seams. Regardless of workmanship, the seams can be detected upon careful inspection of the wall surface, or in certain lighting conditions. Decorating these surfaces with semi-gloss or gloss paint will also magnify the appearance of the drywall joints.

Also, since drywall has some flexibility to it and it is installed over framing lumber (a natural material); portions of the finish surface can seem somewhat irregular. Minor cracks or nail pops may appear and are due to normal shrinkage of the lumber and/or normal settlement of the building. Cracking or separation at drywall and window joints will occur also due to settlement. All of these conditions are considered normal and are not a defect.

MAINTENANCE GUIDELINES

1. Nail pops and minor drywall cracking are normal, especially at wall seams and around windows. IF repairs for minor cracks or nail pops are desired, use Spackle paste or latex caulking. Spread the product with a blade or your finger and then run a moistened towel or sponge over the repair area to smooth and blend with the existing texture. Follow the recommendations of the product regarding drying time and complete the repair with touch-up paint.

ELECTRICAL

MATERIAL CHARACTERISTICS

A panel of circuit breakers protects the electrical wiring and circuits in your home. Circuit breakers are in the electrical panel located on the outside of the home, typically, near the front of the garage. The circuit breakers are labeled to indicate the room(s) or equipment which it controls. Depending on the size of the home, a sub panel may be located in the garage and will usually accommodate the lights/switches/plugs circuits only. The panel and circuit breakers should be identified for you during you New Home Orientation.

The capacity of the service panel has been specified to be more than adequate for daily use. However if you maintain a home office (using a computer, copier, printer, fax, etc.), or have other electrical equipment not found in the typical home, the service may not provide adequate amperage. Overloading (using too many appliances at one time), a defective cord, or starting an electric motor may cause electrical outlet failure. Electric motors require more current when starting, so it is a good idea to turn off a few lights before you turn the motor on.

Each circuit is destined to carry a limited amount of electrical current. If a circuit is overloaded by too many or too powerful an appliance or there is some other malfunction, the circuit breaker will be tripped to the "OFF" position. Before attempting to turn the circuit breaker back on, you should be certain there are no defects in cords or appliances, which draw their current form that circuit. To restore current, simply move the switch to the "ON" position. If power is not restored flip the breaker "OFF" and "ON" once or twice to insure the breaker is rest.

Ground fault Circuit interrupter ("GFCI") outlets are sensitive safety devices installed in the electrical system. The GFCI will "trip" or turn off the circuit if a danger of electrical shock or circuit overload exists. GFCI receptacles are located in water sensitive areas including the kitchen, bathrooms, outdoors, garage, etc. GFCI outlets are designed to "trip" for you protection - this will likely occur from time to time. If the outlet will not reset after a few attempts, do not continue to use the outlet until the "trip" cause is determined.

Do not plug your refrigerator or freezer into a GFCI outlet as it may "trip" due to the surge of the motor. A "tripped" garage outlet could go undetected for quite some time, which could result in food spoilage. If you have an irrigation timer plugged into the GFCI outlet, check the backup battery periodically to ensure power to the clock without disruption.

If there is a complete loss of power to the home, contact your local utility provider directly.

MAINTENANCE GUIDELINES

1. Check the GFCI outlets monthly for proper function. With a small appliance plugged into the GFCI outlet and running press the "test" button. The appliance should shut off. Press the "reset" button and the appliance should start running again. If this does not occur discontinue use of the outlet until the cause of the malfunction can be determined.
2. All lighting fixtures have bulb specifications imprinted on them. For safety and fixture longevity, use only the size and type bulb called for.

3. If you have small children, it is suggested outlets be covered with childproof plastic electrical wall outlet covers.

FANS – CEILING

MATERIAL CHARACTERISTICS

Ceiling fans should come with an explanation of features, care and cleaning requirements and directions. Fans may or may not be provided with your new home. Ceiling fans are considered "consumer products" and are specifically covered by a Manufacturer's warranty. To activate your warranty and service, be sure to complete and mail in the warranty registration cards that are included with your fans.

MAINTENANCE GUIDELINES

1. Because of the fan's natural movement, some connections may become loose. Check the support connections, brackets, and blade attachments frequently and make sure they are secure (it is not necessary to remove the fan from the ceiling to conduct this inspection).
2. Clean your fan periodically to help maintain its new appearance. Make sure the fan is off during cleaning and do not use water when cleaning as this could damage the motor, the wood, or possibly cause an electrical shock.
3. Use only a soft brush or lint-free cloth to avoid scratching the finish. The plating is sealed with a lacquer to minimize discoloration or tarnishing.
4. You can apply a light coat or furniture polish to the wood for additional protection and enhanced beauty.

FENCES/GATES – WOOD

MATERIAL CHARACTERISTICS

Like other wood products on your home, wood fence/gate materials expand with summer heat and contract with winter cold as well as the natural shrinkage which takes place during the normal drying or curing process of the wood. This wood expansion/contraction often causes swelling, drinking, warping, and twisting, cracking and/or separation of joints. All of these conditions are inherent to the natural wood product, and are beyond the control of the Builder.

The wood fence/gate does not have a protective stain or sealer applied to the surface when delivered with the new home. Painting, staining or clear sealing is to be applied and maintained by the Homeowner. Staining or sealing may enhance or preserve the appearance of the new fence, and may extend the life expectancy of the fence. As the wood weathers naturally, it will be subject to staining from weather elements and/or irrigation water.

If altering the original grade of the yard area for the purpose of landscaping, make certain the modified grade is left below the fence. Any wood which is left in contact with the soil will tend to constantly absorb moisture, which can cause the wood to rot. Ground cover, bushes and other plant materials should be trimmed away from the fence so they will not conduct water onto the wood surface.

The posts used to install the fence may be galvanized metal and should not need any maintenance. If the surface is scratched or damaged it is likely the metal will corrode. Otherwise, the metal posts should exceed the life expectancy of the wood fence. If the fence posts are made of wood then they should be preserved in the same fashion as the fence boards.

The constant use of the gate may cause the gate to sag and become misaligned with the latch mechanism over time, and is considered normal wear and tear. The gate may be re-hung with the hinges repositioned, and/or the latch mechanism may be repositioned.

Rear yard fencing installed with the home does not necessarily meet the minimum requirements for pool and spa enclosures. Check with the local building department for code requirements.

Note: If installing sidewalks or patios adjacent to the fencing, closely review your contactor's installation design and specifications and note the height of the finish surface in comparison to the height of the fence. The height of the fence may be shorter than 5' if the concrete is installed on top of the finish grade, as opposed to excavating the soil prior to pouring the concrete. Pay special attention to the finish surface height of your sidewalk so your side-yard access gate will not have to be shortened to accommodate the installation.

MAINTENANCE GUIDELINES

1. Painting, staining or sealing of wood fences and gates are considered to be part of Homeowner maintenance, and should be monitored as needed. Follow the Manufacturer's recommendation

for reapplication in order to maintain the protective coating in order to avoid deterioration to the wood fence.
2. Do not allow landscape sprinklers to spray water directly on the wood fence. Wherever possible, redirect sprinkler heads away from the wood fence. If possible, use drip irrigation in areas adjacent to the fence.
3. Do not build or attach structures or decorations to the fence. The wood fence is not designed to support structures such as woodsheds, storage sheds, and clotheslines, play equipment, etc.
4. Metal gate hinges and lock hasps are fairly low maintenance. Lubrication of the hinges will only be necessary if the operation becomes stiff or becomes squeaky. The gate may need to be re-hung/adjusted over time if the lock hasp does not align properly or the gate is not square in the fence opening.

FENCES – MASONRY WALLS

MATERIAL CHARACTERISTICS

Masonry walls are typically constructed of a cement block core, reinforced with steel rebar or post-tension cable. The masonry block or brick is irregular in size and shape and often has small chips and/or surface cracks. This is normal to the texture of the masonry. The joints between the block/brick will not be perfectly uniform; as the wall is hand laid. Some cracking is normal will all masonry walls, in part because of normal ground movement and temperature changes.

Excessive landscape water will cause the soil to expand and contract, causing movement in the wall footing which can result in cracking. Irrigation water may also cause a harmless but unsightly condition where a dust of white crystal-like material (alkaline) can be seen on the surface of the wall, otherwise known as efflorescence. This is a common occurrence and the removal is part of Homeowner maintenance.

If altering the original grade of the yard area for the purpose of landscaping, make certain the modified grade slopes away from the base of the masonry wall so as not to allow water to pond on the soil over the footing. Although not recommended, if installing a raised planter against a masonry wall, the portion of the wall covered with soil should be waterproofed in order to minimize efflorescence of the opposite side of the wall. An area drain should be installed in the planter in order to remove excess irrigation and rainwater. The raised soil should not exceed 18" in height, as most masonry walls are not engineered to retain soil above 18".

Rear yard fencing and walls installed with the home does not necessarily meet the minimum requirements for pool and spa enclosures. Check with the local building department for code requirements if you are adding these to your yard.

Note: If installing sidewalks or patios adjacent to yard walls, closely review your contractor's installation design and specifications and note the height of the finish surface in comparison to the height of the wall. The height of the wall may be shorter than 5' if the concrete is installed on top of the finish grade, as opposed to excavating the soil prior to pouring the concrete. Pay special attention to the finish surface height of your sidewalk so your side-yard access gate will not have to be shortened to accommodate the installation.

MAINTENANCE GUIDELINES

1. Inspect yard drainage to insure irrigation and rainwater is not allowed to pond against the base of the masonry wall. All runoff water should flow away from the masonry wall.
2. When efflorescence occurs, it may help to spray the affected surface with a mixture of vinegar and water (one part vinegar, four parts water) in a garden sprayer. Any heavy buildup may require scrubbing with a stiff brush and/or the use of a pressure sprayer.
3. Mortar cracks can be repaired with a common mortar mix acquired from any home improvement center.
4. Loose blocks should be removed and the old grout chipped away from the surrounding blocks. New mortar can then be used to reset the original block following the grout Manufacturer's instructions.

FENCES – METAL

MATERIAL CHARACTERISTICS

When used outdoors, metal fencing is finished with a primer and exterior grade enamel paint. However, even with the application of the proper paint primer and enamel paint, rust can develop. Due to exposure to the weather elements and irrigation water, no warranty or guarantee can be made as to the minimum life expectancy of the original paint covering.

Finishes applied to metal fencing will deteriorate quickly. You must give them periodic attention and you should review the condition of the fencing on a regular basis. The original paint will also fade due to exposure to sunlight, and depending on the aging of the original paint, the touchup paint may or may not be an exact match.

Rear yard fencing installed with the home does not necessarily meet the minimum requirements for pool and spa enclosures. Check with the local building department for code requirements.

Note: If installing sidewalks or patios adjacent to the fencing, closely review your contractor's installation design and specifications and note the height of the finish surface in comparison to the height of the fence. The height of the fence may be shorter than 5' if the concrete is installed on top of the finish grade, as opposed to excavating the soil prior to pouring the concrete. Pay special attention to the finish surface height of your sidewalk so your side-yard access gate will not have to be shortened to accommodate the installation.

MAINTENANCE GUIDELINES

1. Do not hang anything on the railing as this may damage the paint coating.
2. Wherever possible, redirect sprinkler heads away from the fence.
3. If possible, use drip irrigation adjacent to the fence.
4. Clean railings as needed to remove common surface dirt with water and a mild household detergent followed by a clear water rinse. Only use a soft brush or broom and low water pressure. Do not use abrasive agents.
5. Water, salty air and chemicals are natural enemies to metal. To prevent corrosion, inspect metal surfaces frequently and touchup/repaint as necessary.
6. When refinishing or touching up the metal fence, use quality paint recommended by the paint manufacturer. Consult with the Manufacturer's dealer or a state licensed painting contractor for surface preparations and paint applications on metal fence surfaces.
7. Lubrication of the hinges on your metal gate will be necessary if the operation becomes still or becomes squeaky. The gatepost may need to be adjusted over time if the lock hasp does not align properly.

FIREPLACE – DIRECT VENT & WOOD BURNING

MATERIAL CHARACTERISTICS

A direct vent fireplace may have been included or purchased with your home. WARNING: A direct vent fireplace is a gas appliance. Do not attempt to burn wood, paper or any other combustible material(s) either with or in place of the manufactured logs included with the fireplace. The appliance does not have a pilot light and it is equipped with a wall switch to turn the flame on/off. Do not try to light the burner by hand.

Before operating the fireplace for the first time, please review the manufacturer's operating instructions. Remember you are operating a gas flame inside your home, so it is important you observe these and all safety measures for fireplace use.

In the event you smell gas, you should be familiar with how to open the access door at the bottom of the fireplace to be able turn the gas line valve off. Review the TROUBLESHOOTING section of this guide for further instructions on action to take should you detect a gas leak and if you have any questions about this you should call your local Gas provider immediately.

When using you fireplace for the first few times, it is normal for the initial paint curing to deposit a slight film on the glass and for you to smell something like dust burning. The film and/or scent may be a result of constituents of natural gas, or dust, lint, etc. which will cling to the surface if condensation should occur. Cleaning of the glass should be all of the maintenance needed. If you notice a smoky scent from this paint burn-off that is a normal occurrence, take care to adequately ventilate the room(s) during the process and the scent should dissipate.

If at any time there is a problem with the flame not igniting, do not attempt to make a repair. Instead, submit a Warranty Service Request to your Builder, or call your local Gas provider to investigate.

If your home has a wood burning fireplace with a log lighter (which is not typically installed by the Builder), you should be careful to initially build low heat fires for the first few times in order to cure the pre-cast panel fireplace lining. If you initially build a very hot fire, intense heat can be generated and cause the fireplace lining to crack; repair or replacement in these cases would not be covered under the warranty. You should avoid burning items such as sawdust, wax logs, newspapers or gift wrapping.

When in use, your fireplace is very hot. Take care in decorating the surrounding areas and avoid contact with the fireplace surfaces that will become hot.

The Builder provides a stub-out for a log lighter pipe addition, however the Homeowner must typically provide and install the log lighter pipe, if desired. A log lighter key is provided to turn the gas on/off if the Homeowner decides to use this feature. Be sure to follow the manufacturer's recommendations and instructions.

MAINTENANCE GUIDELINES

1. As needed, remove the glass door per the manufacturer's instructions for cleaning. When the glass is removed, use the opportunity to vacuum dust, cobwebs, etc. from inside the firebox. Never attempt this when the fireplace is hot.
2. Remove the accumulation of ashes from wood burning fireplaces as often as is necessary. It is best to remove the ashes when they are cool, however always store them in a metal container to reduce the risk of a potential fire if any of the ashes happen to be hot.
3. Check the flue with a flashlight to identify accumulation of soot. Heavy deposits of tar and creosote build-up in the flue may require cleaning by a professional chimney sweep at least once each year or more often depending on usage.

FLOORING – GENERAL

MATERIAL CHARACTERISTICS

Flooring surfaces were likely selected by the Homeowner during the process of purchasing your new home, including carpet and pad, ceramic tile, marble, stone, vinyl and wood.

At the time of purchase, your designer should have provided you with disclosures and specific information on the various flooring products that you have selected. You should take the time to read this important information because it provides guidelines necessary to maintain your manufacturer's warranties as well as care and maintenance suggestions. This information will also provide other specific product information about the warranties on your flooring selections. Please refer to the manufacturer's websites for further information.

It is a good idea to keep your flooring purchase documentation with your other warranty items just in case you need to request warranty service under the manufacturer's warranty. The manufacturer will request this information as proof of purchase and to validate your product warranties.

The uniqueness of material can make replacement and color matching difficult. If warranty service or repair work is required, portions of the original installation may have to be replaced. Your Builder will not be responsible for dye lot variations, discontinued patterns, discontinued ceramic or stone tile sizes, discontinued wood floor materials, lot shade variations, natural or manufactured material variations or grout color variations.

A variety of transition material types are used to separate different types of products. Variance in thickness of any given product will determine the type of transition to be used and reducers, such as vinyl or wood, are often used to help reduce any height difference. The Builder reserves the right to utilize a form of transition and a layout of the transition which best suits the types of flooring materials being installed.

When moving furniture and heavy appliances, lay a plywood panel on the floor and move the item across the panel. This protects your floors from scuffing, tearing and staining. As a general rule, the heavier the item, the more protection you will need.

With vinyl flooring, door not use rubber or latex-backed floor mats or rugs. These products have a potential to cause discoloration to your flooring. Select mats or rugs that are non-staining, are vinyl-backed or woven, and are colorfast. Even certain woven floor rugs may stain your new floor if they become moist or wet. These types of conditions are beyond the control of the Builder and require that the new homeowner pay close attention to prevent these potentially undesirable conditions.

MATERIAL GUIDELINES

1. See Manufacturer's guidelines for instructions on the maintenance of your specific product.

FLOORING – CARPET

MATERIAL CHARACTERISTICS

Carpet is a woven product of multiple layers of nylon and latex and in some cases wool or polypropylene. Refer to the Manufacturer's warranties for stain resistance qualities and warranties; however keep in mind, depending on the type of use and amount of foot traffic, all carpet will stain to some degree regardless of Manufactures' claims or warranties.

Carpet seaming will be selected by the carpet installer to be placed in the most unobtrusive location, depending on the width of the product selected and the dimension of the room where the carpet is installed. This is at the discretion of the installer. Depending on the type of carpet the seam will be more or less noticeable. The visibility of seams is a normal characteristic of carpet, and cannot be completely eliminated. As the carpet ages after the original installation, the seams will tend to relax and will become less noticeable over time.

Also as the carpet ages, it will be susceptible to fading from sunlight. Due to this condition, and the fact the shade color of the carpet will slightly vary from dye lot to dye lot, if a portion of the carpet has to be replaced due to repairs or misuse, the new replacement carpet will not be an exact match to the original carpet.

When the carpet is new, you may notice there will be quite a bit of shedding of loose carpet fibers. This is a normal condition. More frequent vacuuming may be needed at first to relieve this condition. Over time the shedding should abate and a normal vacuuming schedule can them be adhered to.

A special note regarding Berber and pattern carpets, Berber and pattern carpets are installed over a very firm pad of commercial type quality due to the stitching and seams. A perfect match at the seams may not be obtainable and seams are more noticeable with Berber and pattern carpet, especially the cross seams. The natural line of the Berber may not follow the line of the adjacent wall(s). Also, variations in weave may create a slightly wavy appearance, and seams may be more noticeable as a result.

MAINTENANCE GUIDELINES

1. To obtain the best performance and longest wear, adhere strictly to the care and maintenance recommended by the manufacturer, who

has provided you with a care program to help preserve your carpet's appearance during its natural life expectancy.
2. A good vacuum cleaner is vital to prolonging the beauty and life of your carpet. An inexpensive machine can remove the surface dirt but will not effectively remove the hidden dirt and particles embedded in the pile. Most Manufacturers recommend the use of vacuums with a rotating brush or a combination of a beater/brush/bar which agitates the carpet tile and mechanically loosens soil for removal by the vacuum.
3. Initially test your vacuum cleaner in an inconspicuous place, such as in a closet, to find the settings which work the best and are correct for your type of carpet. Settings which are too aggressive for the type of carpet can cause fuzzing or deterioration of the nap. By using the proper setting when you vacuum you can reduce the wear of the carpet.
4. Note: carpet with a thick loop pile construction may be sensitive to brushing or rubbing of the pile surface and may become fuzzy. For these types of carpet products, it is recommended the Homeowner use a vacuum with suction-only or a unit with an adjustable brush lifted away from the carpet so it does not agitate the pile.
5. Remove spots and stains according to Manufacturer's guidelines and as soon as they are discovered.
6. Use doormats at your home's entryways to absorb soil and moisture. Keep in mind all mats will stain if moisture is trapped, and as a result they may cause staining to the underlying surface. An open weave natural fiber type of mat is best.
7. Alter traffic patterns and avoid excessive pile crushing by occasionally moving and rearranging heavy furniture.
8. Protect your carpet from prolonged periods of direct sunlight with window blinds or shades.
9. If you use area rugs over your carpet, remove and clean them regularly, restoring the carpet pile underneath. After cleaning your carpet, always allow for complete drying before replacing the area rugs. Note: area rugs can stain or discolor underlying carpet.
10. Professionally clean your carpet as soon as you notice color dulling. Be sure your carpet cleaning contractor is familiar with the Manufacturers' cleaning guidelines for your specific carpet.

FLOORING – CERAMIC TILE

MATERIAL CHARACTERISTICS

Ceramic tile is a fired of baked clay product with a hard and brittle glaze applied to the surface for color and/or texture. The manufacturer of tile even in modern times remains more of an art than a science. Therefore, even if tile is manufactured to strict tolerances, the individual pieces will still have some inherent flaws. Slight color variations from tile to tile will be typical in genuine glazed ceramic tiles. Also, due to the firing process there may be a slight surface variation, or it may not be perfectly flat. Ceramic tiles with a surface texture will, of course, vary in height.

Grouting the joints between tiles will complete the installation of the ceramic tile countertop. Color grouts for either application may vary in shade from the sample used to select the color due to the wide variety of tiles available, environmental conditions and finishing techniques. The elements of nature, including but not limited to sun, temperature, food or chemical reactions, may combine with aging process to change the color of the grout in varying degrees over time.

Certain areas of colored grout on any given floor area may also vary in color. If repair or replacement of tile or grout areas is required, matching the original or changed color of the remaining colored grout may be impossible. Colored grout can also cause discoloration, flecking and/or cracked appearance of the ceramic tile in the areas where colored grout is used.

Separations and cracks in the grout between the tiles and between those tiles and baseboards, thresholds, backsplashes, bathtubs, shower pans, etc. are considered normal. Repair of cracked grout is a Homeowner maintenance item. The cracks can be repaired with a pre-mixed grout purchased from a paint or hardware store.

Settlement of the house and/or expansion or contraction of the tile substrate may also cause hairline cracks in ceramic tile or grout. This is considered normal.

MAINTENANCE GUIDELINES

1. All ceramic tile surfaces installed in your new home are unsealed. The application of a sealer specifically formulated for use with this

particular material as recommended by the manufacturer is highly advisable. There are several products available with varying Material Characteristics. Follow product instructions for application and maintenance. It is advisable to test an area which is not visible to make sure you are satisfied with the product and the results.
2. Ceramic tile may be cleaned daily with a damp cloth or mop. Extremely dirty areas may be cleaned with a "natural" cleaner and water. Do not use any type of cleansers which contain chemicals or abrasives. Do not use steel wool, acids, or metallic brushes on the tile or grout, as damage may result.
3. No waxing or polishing of ceramic tile is needed. You may use one-half teaspoon full of lemon oil or red oil sprinkled on a soft cloth to remove hard water spots and restore shine to your new tile. Do not do this more frequently than once per month.
4. Always clean up liquid spills and water accumulation as soon as detected, to avoid staining and penetration of moisture through the grout into the substructure.
5. Use doormats at your home's entryways to absorb soil and moisture. Keep in mind all mats will stain if moisture is trapped and as a result they may cause staining to the underlying surface. An open weave natural fiber type of mat is best.
6. If the grout becomes stained, use a mild/diluted bleaching solution or a pre-mixed product, such as Soft Scrub with Bleach. Always rinse thoroughly and wipe with a soft cloth, being careful not to let the bleach solution drip or accumulate onto any adjacent surfaces, which could cause further damage.
7. For colored grouts, color stains are available from ceramic tile stores which can give your grout surface a new appearance.
8. To repair cracked grout between tiles and tiles at baseboard, obtain the proper type and color of grout from a home improvement center. The grout may be available pre-mixed. In either case, follow the manufacturers' instructions for use.
9. Following any grout replacement, wash the area several times with warm water and a sponge to remove the haze residue left behind by the grout.
10. Do not use harsh cleaning agents, steel wool pads, etc., which can scratch or damage the surface of your tile. Be careful not to wash excess grout down the drain, which could cause blockage and cause the need for plumbing repairs.
11. For repair of cracked grout joints at tiled tubs or shower pans, it may be more effective to fill this joint with a silicone-based caulk available from your home improvement store. There may be

repeated movement between the ceramic tile and tub or shower pan due to shrinkage in the framing materials, and a silicone based caulk will maintain flexibility and be less prone to further cracking.

FLOORING – MARBLE AND STONE

MATERIAL CHARACTERISTICS

Marble and natural stone are products of nature, exhibiting unique color and texture variations in each piece, and no two pieces will be exactly the same. Variations of color, shading, veining, thickness and marbling, as well as natural imperfections are all considered normal. Also, because of imperfect quarrying methods the overall dimension of the pieces may not be exact, which will cause variation in the grout lines. Variation in thickness of the pieces will cause height differences between the tiles and is also considered normal.

Marble/natural stones are considered very durable, and although they require little maintenance, periodic upkeep is recommended. Most stones are porous and readily absorb liquids and moisture, and will stain from any topical spill. All acids, including those found in many foods, fruits and beverages will likely etch the surface of polished stone, even if the stone has been sealed. Green marbles are especially susceptible to etching. In bath areas stone surfaces can also be susceptible to discoloration from soap, makeup products and hairsprays.

Grouting the joints between tiles will complete the installation of the ceramic tile floor. Natural gray grout will be relatively uniform in color and is the easiest grout to maintain and repair.

Colored grouts may vary in shade form the sample used to select the color due to the wide variety of tiles available, environmental conditions and finishing techniques. The elements of nature, including but not limited to sun, temperature, food or chemical reactions, may combine with aging process to change the color of the grout in varying degrees over time.

Use of colored grout with a stone surface may cause discoloration of the marble/natural stone due to the porosity of the material. The colored grout may also accentuate normal irregularities of the marble/stone.

Certain areas of colored grout on any given floor area may also vary in color. IF repair or replacement of tile or gout areas is required, matching the original or changed color of the remaining colored grout may be impossible. Colored grout can also cause the discoloration; flecking and/or cracked appearance of the ceramic tile in the areas where colored grout is used.

Separations and cracks in the grout between the tiles and between those tiles and baseboards, thresholds, backsplashes, bathtubs, shower pans, etc. are normal. Repair of cracked grout is a Homeowner maintenance item. The cracks can be repaired with a pre-mixed grout purchased from a paint or hardware store.

Settlement of the house and/or expansion or contraction of the tile substrate may also cause hairline cracks in ceramic tile or grout. This is considered normal.

MAINTENANCE GUIDELINES

1. All marble/natural stone floor surfaces installed in your new home are unsealed. The application of a sealer specifically formulated for use with this particular material as recommended by the manufacturer is highly advisable.
2. If you apply a sealer, it should be one which allows the stone to "breathe." There are several products available. Follow product instructions for applications and maintenance. It is advisable to test an area which is not visible to make sure you are satisfied with the product and the results.
3. Dry mop floors frequently to sweep up dirty and grit. Grit causes scratches on polished marble. Also, particles of asphalt or tar tacked on floors contain oil. Highly alkaline cleaning products are apt to dissolve or emulsify the oily matter and carry it into the marble, causing stains, which are hard to remove.
4. Periodic cleaning of all stone surfaces with warm water is recommended to remove ordinary dirt and dust build up.
5. For more intensive cleaning, consult with the manufacturer of the stone for the type of cleaning product you should use specific to your stone.
6. Avoid the use of cleaning products which have distinctive colors, this includes oil based dressing or colored waxes. Over time, these tend to impart their character into the stone.
7. Avoid cleansers which contain grit or are highly alkaline in composition. Mop and shine products typically obtained off of the grocer's shelf especially are to be avoided as the alkaline will penetrate the surface of the material and then form crystals in the

stone. The pressure exerted by the crystals will pop the stone leaving pits and gouges in the surface.

8. Use doormats at your home's entryways to absorb soil and moisture. Keep in mind all mats will stain if moisture is trapped and as a result they may cause staining to the underlying surface. It is best to place the mats outside the entry doors. An open weave natural fiber type of mat is best, however be careful to select woven mats labeled "colorfast" to prevent the potential of staining from colored dyes used by the manufacturer.
9. Always clean up liquid spills and water accumulations as soon as detected, to avoid staining and penetration of moisture through the grout into the substructure.
10. If the grouting becomes stained, use a mild bleaching solution (diluted to 1 part bleach to 4 parts water). Simply apply a small amount of this mixture and scrub with a soft bristle brush. **Avoid contact of this mixture on the stone.**
11. For colored grouts, color stains are available from ceramic tile stores which can give your grout surface a new appearance. Remember the colored stain may leach into the porous stone.
12. To repair cracked grout between tiles and tiles at baseboard, obtain the proper type and color of grout from a home improvement center. The grout may be available pre-mixed. In either case, follow the manufacturer's instructions for use. After the replacement of the grout, wash the area several times with warm water and a sponge to remove the haze residue left behind the grout.
13. Do not use harsh cleaning agents, steel wool pads, etc., which can scratch or damage the surface of your tile. Be careful not to wash excess grout down the drain, which could cause blockage and cause the need for plumbing repairs.
14. For repair of cracked grout joints at tiled tubs or shower pans, it may be more effective to fill this joint with a silicone-based caulk available from your home improvement store. There may be repeated movement between the ceramic tile and tub or shower pan due to shrinkage in the framing materials, and a silicone based caulk will maintain flexibility and be less prone to further cracking.
15. Do not move heavy objects across marble/natural stone floors as breakage may result. Also, do not use handcarts or any other equipment with wheels on the surface as this may cause scratching, scoring or breakage.

FLOORING – VINYL

MATERIAL CHARACTERISTICS

Vinyl is the softest material of the hard surface floor products and is highly susceptible to dents, scratches, staining and scuffing. Nevertheless, it is effective flooring and is often used in areas where water and spills are likely, such as the kitchen, laundry and bath areas.

This type of flooring material will provide years of service when properly maintained. Pay close attention to the Manufacturer's Warranty and Care and Maintenance Guidelines. Vinyl flooring can be susceptible to heavy usage so proper care is crucially important.

MAINTENANCE GUIDELINES

1. Sweep or vacuum frequently to prevent dirt particles from being ground into the surface of the vinyl flooring.
2. Wipe up spills immediately to avoid staining.
3. To clean, use a damp mop and clean water to lightly wash the flooring surfaces weekly. If desired use one teaspoon of vinegar or Windex mixed with each gallon of water.
4. IF the flooring surfaces receive hard use and become extremely dirty, use a mild detergent in the mop water, and apply the detergent solution to the floor with a sponge mop. After the soil deposits have been loosened, mop up excess detergent and water. Rinse the mop thoroughly with clear water to remove all of the detergent, and then rinse the floor using the clean mop with fresh, warm water to remove the soapy residue. Any detergent film left on the floor can hold tracked-in dirt and leave the surface with a dull, cloudy appearance.
5. Avoid solvent-based cleaners, abrasive cleaners, or wax.
6. Do not use rubber-backed or latex-backed floor rugs or mats on your vinyl floors. These products may potentially stain or discolor your vinyl flooring. Refer to the tags on your rugs for labeling such as "colorfast" and "non-staining"; these qualities will prevent potential problems with discoloration.
7. Use doormats at your home's entryways to absorb soil and moisture. Keep in mind all mats will stain if moisture is trapped and as a result they may cause staining to the underlying surface. An open weave natural fiber type of mat is best.

8. Avoid the wearing of pointed or black heels on vinyl flooring. The concentrated weight will leave dents in the surface and black heels may stain or mark the surface.
9. Exposure to direct sunlight on your floor for prolonged periods can cause fading. During peak sunlight hours, the use of drapes or blinds is recommended.
10. Protect your floor against burns from cigarettes, matches and extremely hot items.
11. Resilient-flooring material will tear if heavy appliances, such as refrigerators, washers or dryers, are improperly moved across the surface. Use appropriate appliance dollies. Heavy furniture should be placed on pads to avoid point loads, such as sofa legs or piano legs, from penetrating the surface.
12. If installed in a bathroom, inspect the joint between the vinyl flooring and the toilet as well as the joint between the flooring and the tub or shower on a monthly basis. Touchup any gaps or shrinkage in the caulking as needed.

FLOORING – WOOD

MATERIAL CHARACTERISTICS

Wood floor material is a product of nature and will contain natural imperfections. The material has been manufactured in accordance with accepted industry standards. Imperfections may be a result of manufacturing (within acceptable tolerances) or it may be a natural characteristic of the wood. The Industry accepted stains, waxes, fillers or putty sticks will be used for cosmetically correcting imperfections during installation of the floor.

Height variation may occur between floorboards due to a difference in material heights and sub-floor undulation. Separation between boards may also vary due to temperature and humidity related expansion and contraction.

Mod wood floor material used today is laminate flooring. Laminate flooring is a high-pressured engineered composite, consisting of layers of wood fused together to provide a wear and impact resistant surface. The core layer resists swelling and indentation and provides stability. The backing provides structural balance and added strength. The tongue and groove bonding is a floating floor installation system. This floating floor installation may flex and create a hollow sound when walked on. The floor will be installed per the Manufacturer's requirements, and the proper installation may include the separation of large areas with a T-molding to allow for proper expansion and contraction.

All laminate flooring is susceptible to dents, cracks and scratches. Scratches cannot be rejuvenated like a solid wood floor. To protect the floor from scratching, follow the maintenance guidelines from the flooring manufacturer.

Please note pre-finished wood floors will not match the stain on other items such as cabinets.

MAINTENANCE GUIDELINES

1. Vacuum or dust mop at the same frequency as for carpeting.
2. A damp (not a wet) mop can be used for spills on floors which have a non-waxed polyurethane finish (always follow the damp mop with a dry cloth to insure no moisture is left on the wood surface).
3. Some scuffing should be expected in areas of heavy traffic. If the floor is waxed, occasional buffing helps remove scuffmarks. A waxed floor should only be re-waxed per the recommendations provided by the manufacturer.
4. No matter what type of finish is on your wood floor, never intentionally pour water directly on the floor. While damp mopping is fine for non-waxed polyurethane finishes in good condition, excessive amounts of water may find a way of seeping between the boards, causing stains or warping (always follow the damp mop with a dry cloth to insure no moisture is left on the wood surface).
5. Use doormats at your home's entryways to absorb soil and moisture. Keep in mind that all mats will stain if moisture is trapped and as a result they may cause staining to the underlying surface. An open weave natural fiber type of mat is best.
6. Avoid the wearing of high heels on wood flooring. The concentrated weight will leave dents in the surface.
7. Exposure to direct sunlight on your floor for prolonged periods can cause fading. During peak sunlight hours, the use of drapes or blinds is recommended.
8. Throw rugs or area rugs left in one location for an extended period of time may cause discoloration or uneven fading to the wood finish.
9. Protect your floor against burns from cigarettes, matches and extremely hot items.

10. Wood flooring material will dent and/or splinter if heavy appliances, such as refrigerators, washers or dryers, are improperly moved across the surface. Use appropriate appliance dollies.
11. At a minimum all furniture placed on wood floors should use felt protectors on furniture legs. Heavy furniture should be placed on pads to avoid point loads, such as sofa legs or piano legs, from indenting the surface.

FOOD DISPOSAL

MATERIAL CHARACTERISTICS

Your disposal is self-cleaning and self-contained, needing no maintenance or lubrication of the motor. Because it is a consumer product, you must complete and mail in the warranty registration card for service. For optimum performance with the least amount of wear and tear, run plenty of cold water when using the disposal.

If the disposal will not start, follow the instructions as provided by the manufacturer in combination with the following information.

MAINTENANCE GUIDELINES

1. Always use cold water when the disposal is operating
2. Use the disposal sparingly to maximize the disposal life.
3. Do not grind extremely fibrous food materials such as certain meats, vegetables and fruit rinds, artichokes, celery or cornhusks as they will plug the drain and may cause a blockage or jam of the disposal.
4. To clean the disposal, fill the sink with cold water, turn on the disposal and remove the stopper. While the water is draining through the disposal, allow the tap to continue running. When the sink is empty, the disposal will be clean.
5. Odors can be caused over time by accumulation of food particles or grease in the grind chamber. This buildup may be a result of insufficient water flow during and after use of the disposal.
6. The disposal unit can be "freshened up" with a small ice cubes which are a solution of one (1) cup of vinegar per tray of water. Start the disposal and add a tray of vinegar ice cubes. After the grinding action is completed, flush the disposal with cold water. Grinding lemon peels will also help with masking odors.

7. Never put lye or other chemical drainpipe cleaners into the disposal unit, as they will cause serious corrosion of any alloy parts. This will also void all guarantees and warranties.

OPERATING GUIDELINES

1. Do not overload the disposal
2. Always operate the disposal with the splashguard in place and according to the manufacturer's operating and troubleshooting instructions.
3. Before calling for service you should check the following:
   a. Loud noises- when the unit and water is completely off, remove the splash guard, as needed, and use tongs to investigate for and remove any foreign objects. Replace the splashguard. Never insert your hand into the disposal.
   b. Unit does not start or is jammed- Use the hex wrench provided with the unit to reverse the disposal teeth. The hex nut is located under the disposal unit. When the disposal turns freely, push the red reset button and then turn the disposal on.
      i. If the previous effort is unsuccessful, check with a screwdriver or broom handle to see if the turntable inside the unit rotates freely
      ii. If the turntables move freely, check the reset button. If it has been tripped, push it back in until you hear a click, and it remains depressed. If the rest button is not tripped, check the following in this order: a) shorted or broken wire connected to the unit; b) wall switch for loose connection; c) fuse box/circuit breaker. Further action will require a qualified repair person to keep the warranty intact.
      iii. If the turntable is stuck, check for a foreign object lodged between the turntable and the grind ring. Dislodge by rotating turntable with a pry bar, screw driver, de-jamming tool or broom handle. Remove the foreign object. Further action will require a qualified repair person to keep the warranty intact.

FRAMING

MATERIAL CHARACTERISTICS

Wood expands with summer heat and contracts with winter cold as well as the natural shrinkage which takes place during normal drying (curing) process. This often causes minor swelling, shrinking, warping, twisting, cracking and or separation of joints in framing members, which is beyond the control of the framing contractor or Builder. Realizing these material characteristics, your home has been professionally engineered with these factors in mind.

To maintain the structural integrity of your new home, do not alter or misuse specific engineered design components. If you wish to remodel your home, do so only under the guidance of a qualified State licensed structural engineer and architect. You should also check with the local Building Dept. to see if any permits and inspections will be required for the work being performed.

If you need structural information regarding your home, you can check with the local Building Dept. The approved building plans are on file and are a matter of public record.

Walls: The inner and outer walls of your home are made up of a system which includes wood posts, steel posts, wood beams, and an engineered steel reinforced foundation with wood-to-wood connectors, and shear paneling. Because of structural design requirements, many of the walls of your home are considered structural or "bearing" walls. Improper modification to the individual framing components could cause possible structural damage or failure.

Roof Trusses/Attic: The roof trusses in your home have been designed specifically to carry the weight load of the roof sheathing and roof material (tile, shingles, etc.), as well as any mechanical equipment installed in the attic area. The trusses are not engineered to carry any additional weight (household goods, support sheathing for storage, etc.). DO NOT USE ROOF TRUSSES/ATTIC FOR STORAGE!

Second Story Floors: The second story floor is also a structural component to the entire home. The floor system of a typical home is not designed to support the weight load of a waterbed, a piano, a pool table or heavy exercise equipment. If you decide to place any of these heavy objects in a second story area at your own risk, then you should consider placing floor coasters under each furniture leg or foot in order to spread the weight load of the heavy object. This may help prevent a puncture to the wood floor sheathing.

Your floors may squeak from time to time because of drying wood, weather, uneven temperature inside and normal settling.

MAINTENANCE GUIDELINES

1. During the first heating season, try to keep interior temperatures no warmer than 68-70 degrees. High temperatures will tend to dry the wood in your home too quickly which can increase warping, twisting and cracking.
2. Exterior exposed wood should be checked frequently to assure satisfactory condition of the paint/stain. To avoid damage to the wood, touchup or repaint as necessary.

GARAGE DOORS (SECTIONAL ROLL-UP)

MATERIAL CHARACTERISTICS

The typical sectional roll-up garage door is made of metal, including the frame, tracks, panels, etc. The panels have been pre-finished with a baked on paint finish. This finish is very low maintenance. Scratches in the surface can cause corrosion. If scratches occur they should be lightly sanded and then touched up with a spray primer and paint. It may be difficult to match the original paint due to fading.

The panels are similar to a car door. Bumping the panel may cause a dent. Never use the door surface as a backstop for sports play.

The manufacturer guarantees the garage doors installed in your home. This warranty does not apply if the garage door(s) are misused, altered or used for any purpose other than normal household use. The garage door openers are also a consumer product and must be registered by sending a completed warranty registration card, to the manufacturer.

Check the Manufacturer's instructions for complete operating, maintenance and safety instructions.

Note: Be sure to disconnect the electrical garage door opener prior to performing any repair work. Pull the red Emergency Release Knob to release door from the rail assembly if you need to raise or lower the door manually (instructions are on the release knob tag). To re-engage the door with the rail, pull the red Emergency Release Knob toward the motor. Do not attempt to open the door with the inside manual security lock engaged. To do so may cause irreparable damage to the door.

MAINTENANCE GUIDELINES

1. Visually inspect the garage door springs, cables, chains, pulleys and other door hardware for signs of wear. If the door and/or opener are under warranty, contact the installation contractor directly to schedule any necessary repairs.
2. The Homeowner should conduct maintenance of the complete garage door system on a monthly basis. Safety is everyone's business and garage door safety should become automatic. Refer to the manufacturer's safety and maintenance guidelines for safe and trouble-free operation, however at a minimum, monthly maintenance should include the following;
    a. Oil the door rollers, bearings, and hinges with a silicone lubricant or light oil.
    b. Check the door balance by releasing the door from the rail assembly and manually raising door to approximately 3 feet. If the door does not stay in this position then have the door serviced by a professional.
    c. Perform the CONTACT REVERSE inspection as described in the operating instructions. If the operator fails the test then have the door serviced by a professional.
3. Once a year the Homeowner should complete the following in accordance with the manufacturer's guidelines;
    a. Lubricate the drive screw using only "Lubriplate" Low Temperature grease. Other lubricants may damage the operator.
4. When dirty, the door panel surfaces can be washed with a mild detergent and rinsed off with a garden hose using normal house water pressure (do not use a pressure sprayer as it may peel the paint from the surface).
5. An automobile wax can be periodically used to freshen the appearance of the door, and may help to prolong the life expectancy of the finish.

GAS METER

MATERIAL CHARACTERISTICS

Be prepared for emergencies. Know where your gas meter is located and have a 10" or 12" adjustable wrench with your emergency supplies. In an emergency such as an earthquake, turn off your gas meter only if you smell gas or hear the hissing sound of gas escaping.

If you shut off the gas, call your local Gas provider when the emergency is over to have your meter turned on and your appliances inspected. Do not attempt to restore your own service—there may be leaks, or pilot valves left unlit and in the "ON" position.

MAINTENANCE GUIDELINES

1. Please contact your local Gas provider if you experience any problems with the gas service.

HVAC – AIR CONDITIONING

MATERIAL CHARACTERISTICS

If your home has been equipped with air conditioning as part of the HVAC system, the system has been designed to meet the heating and cooling requirements of your home, as well as meeting any State energy efficiency requirements.

You can expect a certain amount of noise from the system. This is due to air movements, expansion and contraction of metal ducts, or the motor, fan and other moving parts of the system.

The manufacturer may offer warranty coverage on equipment parts and equipment labor, so make sure to check the literature. For a fee, the original installation contractor may provide additional coverage on the HVAC system, including some parts and labor so make sure to check the literature. If you are interested in an extended warranty, please contact the installation contractor directly or your Builder's Customer Service Department for a referral.

Typically, during the first thirty (30) days after taking possession of your home, your Builder's Customer Service Department will gladly schedule a

Service Representative to come to your home to demonstrate removal, cleaning and replacing of air filters, which is considered a part of normal Homeowner maintenance.

Periodically there will be a question or concern as to whether multiple AC condenser units that have been installed are not the same size or otherwise do not appear to be the same as the secondary condenser in size, color or have some other difference. The AC condensers installed on your home meet the local Energy and engineering requirements, but may not be the exactly the same equipment.

MAINTENANCE GUIDELINES

1. Prior to moving into your new home it is a good idea to run the unit for several hours as a minor amount of dust from the installation process will likely be circulated through the new ducting system. This dust will be eliminated after the unit is run for the first time. It is also a good idea to open some windows during this time to help freshen up the air.
2. A dirty air filter will decrease airflow and will restrict heating and cooling capability. This causes the equipment to operate much longer in order to reach the desired temperature and will increase operating costs. At a minimum the filter should be cleaned or replaced in accordance with the manufacturer's instructions. For optimum performance, clean or replace the filters at more frequent intervals.
3. As with any piece of sophisticated machinery, the HVAC system should be cleaned and checked periodically by a professional service contractor. Mark the inspection dates recommended by the manufacture on your calendar. Schedule all work on your equipment early in the spring to avoid delays during peak demand periods.
4. This is a consumer product and you must complete and mail in the warranty registration card.

OPERATING GUIDELINES

For optimum performance:

- Clean or replace the air filters monthly during the air-conditioning season

- For optimum cooling, close up the house earlier in the day. This will avoid the system having to work harder to cool down the house after it has been allowed to become extremely hot.
- Set the thermostat at the desired temperature.
- If a warmer room is desired partially close the register(s) in that room.
- Conserve energy and reduce heating costs by closing off registers to rooms not in use.
- Turn off lights when they are not needed and close or angle the window coverings to keep out direct sunlight. These measures will help keep the house cooler.
- With the changing of the seasons and demands on your cooling system, the registers should be adjusted to provide the desired temperature for each room as well as balancing the temperature through the house.
- Install patio covers, awnings, trees, and bushes at large glass areas on ground floors with south/western exposure.

TROUBLESHOOTING

If your system is not cooling properly, check:

- Is the thermostat set below room temperature?
- Is the thermostat selector set on "cool"?
- Has a circuit breaker controlling your cooling system been tripped?
- Are the filters clogged?
- Have the cooling coils iced up?

CONDENSATION

At times the cooling coils may ice up due to high humidity conditions. This is a normal condition. Turn the system OFF and allow the ice to melt before turning the system back on, 1-2 hours is typical. If the cooling does not return to acceptable levels, turn the unit OFF and contact your Builder's Customer Service Department as soon as possible.

Secondary condensate lines have been installed at the condensate pan to divert water if the primary condensate line has become plugged or otherwise disabled. The outlet for the secondary condensate has been placed over a window; malfunction of the primary condensate will bring water trickling from the secondary condensate outlet and down in front of the window. If this occurs, something is wrong with the primary condensate line and the condensate pan may overflow. This could cause drywall and paint damage to the ceiling under the air-conditioning equipment. Turn off the air-conditioner and check the condensate lines and the condensate pan. Do not re-start the air-conditioner without identifying and resolving the problem. You may need to contact a qualified service technician if this occurs.

HVAC – HEATING

MATERIAL CHARACTERISTICS

Your home is equipped with a Heating, Ventilating and (optional) Air Conditioning system (HVAC). The system has been designed to meet the heating and cooling requirements of your home, as well as meeting with your local energy efficiency requirements.

You can expect a certain amount of noise from the system. This is due to air movements, expansion and contraction of metal ducts or the motor, fan and other moving parts of the system. Ticking or cracking noises will occur when the metal ductwork expands and contracts as warm and cold air circulates through it.

The forced air unit (furnace) may smoke for a brief period when first put into service. This is due to the dust particles inside the heater and the freshness of new paint. There may also be a slight odor, which should disappear in a few minutes, when operating your heater for the first time or at the beginning of the winter season.

If your heater is a gas furnace, the in-line shutoff valve should be demonstrated to you during your New Home Orientation. If the heater smells like it is leaking gas, turn the valve perpendicular to the line to the "OFF" position and ventilate the area. Follow the instructions in the TROUBLESHOOTING GUIDE for contacting your local Gas provider. If you still smell a gas odor after turning off the in-line valve and ventilating the area, turn off the main supply to the house at the gas meter.

The manufacturer may offer warranty coverage on equipment parts and equipment labor, so make sure to check the literature. For a fee, the original installation contractor may provide additional coverage on the HVAC system, including some parts and labor so make sure to check the literature.

If you are interested in an extended warranty, please contact the installation contractor directly.

Typically, during the first thirty (30) days after taking possession of your home, your Builder's Customer Service Department will gladly schedule a Service Representative to come to your home to demonstrate removal, cleaning and replacing of air filters, which is considered a part of normal Homeowner maintenance.

MAINTENANCE GUIDELINES

1. Prior to moving into your new home it is a good idea to run the unit for several hours as a minor amount of dust from the installation process will likely be circulated through the new ducting system. This dust will be eliminated after the unit is run for the first time. It is also a good idea to open some windows during this time to help freshen up the air.
2. The Forced Air Unit (FAU) houses the fan which blows air through the system. The areas around your forced air unit must be kept clean and completely free of any combustible or flammable materials.
3. A dirty air filter will decrease airflow and heating capability. This causes the equipment to operate much longer in order to reach the desired temperature (which in the case of an extremely dirty filter may never happen) and will increase operating costs. At a minimum the filter should be cleaned or replaced every three months. For optimum performance at lowest operating cost and less wear and tear to your equipment, monthly cleaning or replacement is best.
4. As with any piece of sophisticated machinery, the HVAC system, especially filter, should be checked periodically and cleaned by a professional service contractor. Mark inspection dates recommended by the manufacturer on your calendar. Schedule all work on your equipment early in fall to avoid delays during peak demand periods.
5. The motor and bearing in blower-type units should be oiled only if recommended by the manufacturer.
6. This is a consumer product and you must complete and mail in the warranty registration.

OPERATING GUIDELINES

For optimum performance:

- Clean or replace the air filters monthly during heating season.
- Set thermostat at desired temperature and leave it there.
- Setting a lower temperature at night will save energy costs, utilize the night set-back feature of your thermostat to automatically adjust the temperature range during a 24 hour period
- If a cooler room is desired partially close register(s) in that area.
- Conserve energy and reduce heating costs by closing off registers to rooms not in use.
- With the changing of the seasons and demands on your heating system, registers should be adjusted to provide the desired temperature for each room as well as balancing the temperature through the house.

TROUBLESHOOTING

If your system is not heating properly, check:

- Is the thermostat set above room temperature?
- Is the thermostat selector set on "heat"?
- Has a circuit breaker controlling your heating system been tripped?
- Is the gas shutoff turned to the ON position?
- Are the filters clogged?

LANDSCAPE AND IRRIGATION

Maintenance of landscaping and irrigation systems installed by the Builder is the responsibility of the Homeowner.

MAINTENANCE GUIDELINES

1. Watering:
    a. Always consult a Landscape Professional for watering and fertilization requirements for your custom landscaping.
    b. Water your yard but don't over water it! Factors which contribute to water needs are the type of turf grass (cool season grasses use most water) and location in the yard

(shady areas need less water), the climate and the variation in soils, including the amendments.

c. To water, turn on only one valve at a time. Soil may be expansive, which means if it becomes over saturated it will expand or conversely it will contract if it becomes too dry. These occurrences can cause movement in the foundation of the home or your landscape improvements, and contribute to cracking, etc.
d. Avoid watering at night or very late afternoon, as this may promote fungus in the lawn.
e. Water less when skies are cloudy or when the weather is cool. If it rains, watering should be reduced or skipped.
f. Gradually decrease the amount of water in the fall as winter rains approach. In winter, water only during warm or extended dry periods.
g. Water less in permanently shaded areas.
h. During the rainy season, reduce or cease irrigating if possible. Gradually adjust the amount of water over the spring season to reach the summer water needs.
i. Watch for visual signs of under watering, such as dry spots or wilting, especially during hot or windy weather.
j. Avoid watering sidewalks, patios and streets. If water is flowing off the grass into the gutter and your system is divided into multiple valves, either reduce the amount of watering time or set your timer to divide the watering time into two blocks. This will allow the soil to accept the applied water.
k. In areas with deep, sandy soil, water may percolate below the grass root zone. Compensate by dividing the watering time into two blocks.
l. Small lawns surrounded by concrete or other heat-reflecting urban structures may require slightly more water than open-lawn areas.
m. Do not allow sprinklers to spray water on the surfaces of your home. The water will result in blisters and peeling of paint, causing wood to warp, discolor, dry out and splinter, or for stucco surfaces to mold and deteriorate prematurely.
n. As bushes and plants mature, they may grow in a manner which will block the spray from sprinkler heads. If the plants cannot be trimmed sufficiently, it may be necessary to raise or move the sprinkler heads to maintain proper coverage.

o. Excessive watering of shrubs against a block wall may cause cracks in the wall.
p. Maintain a large enough water basin around plants so enough water can be applied to establish moisture through the major root zone.

2. Irrigation System: Check the system often for proper operation. Some Homeowners may need the assistance of a professional landscape maintenance contractor to check the system and keep the components in the proper condition, as follows:
   a. Check and flush 1/2 inch polyethylene lines once every month.
   b. Check and clean filters once every month.
   c. Check the drip emitters/sprinklers once every monthly for proper operation.
   d. Clear weed growth from around emitter/sprinkler areas.
   e. Check exposed tubing for leaks and kinking.
   f. Check pressure regulator for correct pressure setting (PSI).
   g. Check controller program for correction operation. Adjust the automatic controller program (four times per year) to accommodate seasonal water requirements. Replace the battery periodically to insure interrupted operation in the event of a power failure.
3. Mow and edge you lawn weekly or as often as necessary to maintain a healthy appearance. The "typical" proper cut height for **cool-season turf**, such as fescue or Kentucky bluegrass should be between 2 1/2 - 4 inches, and between 1 - 3 inches for **warm-season grasses**, including zoysia and Bermuda grass.
4. Fertilize lightly each month with a quality all-purpose tree/shrub/groundcover and/or turf fertilizer. Follow the manufacturer's instructions for application and follow-up watering. Use products which are recommended for your climate and specific to seasonal applications.
5. Apply products for weed prevention and removal as necessary and avoid frequent cultivation as it destroys shallow roots, especially in ground cover areas. There are products available which fertilize and prevent weed growth simultaneously.

PAINTED SURFACES – EXTERIOR

MATERIAL CHARACTERISTICS

The chemical composition of all paint is affected by climatic conditions; exposure to sun, rain, wind, fog, dew and water. Over time, the finish might crack, chip, peel and/or fade. This is a natural aging process and cannot be stopped. For a consistent color match when repainting, have your paint supplier or home improvement center color match with a chip taken from the surface you are planning on touching up or repainting.

It should be noted because of the aging process the paint color will be constantly changing. In the event warranty service repair is performed on the exterior of your home which will require touchup paint, the original paint color will be used by the Builder to complete the work. Color or shade matching of the repaired area to the adjacent original painted surfaces is not guaranteed.

Variations in wood grain on natural wood trim will affect the appearance of the finish coat of paint. The variations to the wood finish are inherent material characteristics contributing to the surface appearance of these architectural features, and cannot be controlled.

MAINTENANCE GUIDELINES

1. The exterior surface of your home may have exposed wood, which has been painted according to industry standards. You can maintain its appearance by frequently removing surface dust and dirt.
2. No absolute schedule for painting can be established as the weather, wind and sun exposure affect building surfaces differently. The exterior of the home should be inspected at least once per year to observe aging and to make any necessary touchups. If the paint is given a chance to deteriorate, moisture will begin to penetrate the wood and will cause damage.
3. Remember exposure to the sun and other weather elements will cause fading and the new touchups may not match exactly.
4. Do not allow landscaping sprinklers to spray water on the exterior finish surfaces of your home. Continuous contact with water causes deterioration of painted or stained surfaces.

5. If you decide to repaint the exterior of your home, choose a state licensed painting contractor who is expert in surface preparation and applications.
6. Exterior doors that are typically finished with gloss, or semi-gloss paint, are very difficult to touch-up. For best appearance it may be necessary to prepare and repaint the entire door at once.
7. If mold or mildew appears on any painted surface, it is important to locate and remedy the source. Contact your Builder's Customer Service Department for assistance if this condition should occur.
8. **Important Note:** Remember your CC&R's may restrict the colors which can be applied to the exterior of your home. If your neighborhood is governed by an HOA and you wish to make changes to the exterior color scheme, reference the CC&R's for instructions on submitting a color scheme change request. It will be up to the Architectural Review Committee to review and approve the request.

PAINTED SURFACES – INTERIOR

MATERIAL CHARACTERISTICS

The walls, woodwork and other interior painted components of your home have been painted with the appropriate type of paint product depending upon their use. It is typical for the woodwork, kitchen walls, bathroom walls and utility room walls have been painted with semi-gloss paint. All other walls have been painted with interior flat paint.

Your home may include stain grade woods in some locations such as for stairs, entry doors, etc. Unlike furniture building, in the construction of homes the stain grade wood components are not matched for similarities. It is expected there will be variations in hardness, grain and color of the natural wood and the species of woods may not even be specified to match between the entry door, stair railing, cabinets, etc. These variations will dictate how the stain will reappear on the finished surface. The finish may not necessarily be even in appearance. Also, color matching between wood parts and components cannot be guaranteed even when using the same stain color. These variations are natural material characteristics of real wood.

The chemical composition of all paint and stain is affected by climatic conditions. Over time, the finish might fade, dull and/or yellow. This is a natural aging process. You may find the kitchen and baths require more frequent re-painting than the rest of your home due to steam condensation and more frequent usage. For a consistent color match when repainting or refinishing, have your paint supplier or home improvement center color match with a chip taken from the surface you are planning to touch up or repaint.

When you redecorate or repaint the interior of the home, you should re-review and keep in mind the material characteristics of drywall. As previously noted, drywall will have some inherent flaws and blemishes which are considered normal; seams or joints which are noticeable, slight wave or unevenness in the wallboard, uneven texture, etc. When a flat paint is applied to the walls it tends to de-emphasize the inconsistencies in the drywall finish as flat paint absorbs light instead of reflecting it. If these surfaces are painted with a semi-gloss or gloss paint, the inconsistencies in the drywall will be accentuated due to the light reflection. If a semi-gloss or gloss finish is desired, you should consult with a professional painter to properly prepare the surface and minimize the inconsistencies.

MAINTENANCE GUIDELINES

1. A move-in paint kit is typically supplied with your new home and contains enough paint to make minor touch ups to the interior paint. It is a good idea to keep these cans after the paint is gone and to make a note listing the paint manufacturer and paint codes so you can purchase additional paint at a later date.
2. On painted or laminated surfaces use only a mild soap with warm water for necessary cleaning. Do not use brushes or abrasives, which can scratch or remove paint.
3. Minor cracks at room corners or around windows and doors are normal and are part of Homeowner maintenance out outlined in the DRYWALL section of this guide. Following the technique suggested for repair of minor cracks, it is possible paint touchup can be avoided.
4. Flat wall paint may not be necessarily washable. Before washing a large area which is needed, it is a good idea to experiment with washing on an area which is not highly visible such as in a closet.

PEST CONTROL

MATERIAL CHARACTERISTICS

Pest control is an issue related to nature and is beyond the control of your Builder. If you encounter a problem with pests, contract a professional pest control company.

PLUMBING – FAUCETS

MATERIAL CHARACTERISTICS

Refer to the PRODUCT LITERATURE & MANUFACTUER'S WARRANTIES section for terms of the Warranty on your faucets. Contact your Builder's Customer Service Department if you have questions about the type(s) of faucets installed in your home.

The best way to prolong faucet life is to avoid force when turning off the water. Unnecessary force may cut or otherwise damage "O" rings, washers, sleeves or seats and require premature replacement of the entire faucet. Normal hand pressure should result in a full shutoffs of water flow and drips. Loose or worn washers usually cause noisy pipes and faucets, as well as drips.

If your sink faucet has a removal spray nozzle, take car to never let water flow back into the opening where the nozzle is seated. This situation could possibly occur when filling large pots, pans, fish bowls, etc. and if the sink if used for bathing of children, pets or otherwise. Water entering through the opening may potentially damage contents in the cabinet below of the cabinet itself. You should take care to prevent this situation as damage to the cabinet or contents will not be repaired or replaced by your builder under the warranty.

If a sink faucet develops a leak, turn the water valve stop to the OFF position. The water valve stop is located underneath the sink. **For a tub or shower faucet leak within the wall, turn off the house water supply at the main valve control and notify your Builder's Customer Service Department or a professional plumber, as appropriate.** Shutoff valve locations should have been demonstrated to you at your New Home Orientation. Please call your Builder's Customer Service Department if you have any questions regarding these locations.

MAINTENANCE GUIDELINES

1. Use only a soft cloth to clean and shine all handles and decorative finishes. Using polish, detergents, abrasive cleaners, organic solvents or acid may cause damage.
2. Replace valve gaskets, as necessary, disassembling the faucet according to the Manufacturer's guidelines. Use only specified replacement parts for repairs. **Note:** Always turn-off the water supply and relieve pressure before working on your faucet.
3. A leaking faucet may result from a worn out washer or from excessive sediment collected on the valve seat. Replacement stem assembly cartridges can be purchased at any plumbing supply store.
4. Remove (unscrew) the aerator (the screen device located where the water exists the faucet) and flush out any foreign objects to maintain a smooth water flow every six (6) months, or as necessary.
5. If the water heater, garden or washing machine faucet valves leak at the base of the handle, tighten the packing nut located on the top of the valve and add more packing if needed.

PLUMBING – HOT WATER HEATER

MATERIAL CHARACTERISTICS

Your water heater is fully warranted by the manufacturer. The Manufacturers' limited warranty is void is the water heater is misused, altered or used for anything other than normal private household use. Long showers or filling a large tub can deplete the supply of hot water and it may take an hour or more to restore the hot water supply. The situation is not considered a defect of the hot water heater.

Your water heater system is equipped with a relief valve safety feature which helps prevent damage from excessive pressure or temperature. The strapping secures the tank in the event of an earthquake, or any kind of movement, and should not be modified or removed. Always keep the area around your water heater clear and free from dirt, debris, flammables and storage items.

In the event of a leak in the hot water heater or connections you should contact a plumber.

If your water heater is fueled by natural gas, the in-line shutoff valve should be demonstrated to you during your New Home Orientation. If the hot water heater smells like it is leaking gas, turn the valve perpendicular to the line to the "OFF" position and ventilate the area. Follow the instructions in the TROUBLESHOOTING GUIDE for contacting your local Gas provider. If you still smell a gas odor after turning off the in-line valve and ventilating the area, turn off the main supply to the house at the gas meter.

You may notice a ticking noise as your water heater goes through a heating cycle. This is normal, resulting from the differing expansion and contraction rates of the inner and outer walls which protect the piping used to vent the heater. This vent's location is determined by the home design; it must be in the wall closest to the top of the water heater in two-story homes, otherwise it is vented directly into the attic space. This is a consumer product and you must complete and mail in the warranty registration card in order to obtain service.

MAINTENANCE GUIDELINES

1. Regularly inspect your water heating equipment, including the temperature control (110F maximum) and pressure relief valve function. Make repairs and adjustments as necessary.
2. Plan for an annual inspection of the water heater by a properly licensed technician. Ideally this can be completed simultaneously with an inspection of your HVAC system (furnace and/or air-conditioning equipment). This inspection and service should be in accordance with the manufacturer's recommendations.

OPERATION GUIDELINES

- **"Normal"** is the recommended thermostat setting for everyday use. If you need more heat than is provided by the "normal" setting, set the thermostat to **"hot"** and reset for everyday use. Follow all manufacturer supplied operation, maintenance and safety information at all times.
- To re-light the heater, remove the pilot cover plate, turn the control knob located on the front of the unit to "PILOT", depress the red button and light the pilot while holding the red button down for thirty (30) seconds. Release. Replace the cover plate and turn the control knob to "ON". The water heater should then self-light. Be sure to read the lighting instructions in the instruction manual before attempting to light the pilot.
- NEVER light a gas pilot or turn on electricity when the water heater tank is empty. Always turn off the gas supply at the water

heater before shutting off the cold water supply. Instructions for lighting the pilot are usually found on the burner near the pilot access opening. Read the instructions before trying to light the gas pilot. Consult a qualified service contractor, or your local Gas provider if you have any other questions.

PLUMBING – PORCELAIN FIXUTRES

MATERIAL CHARACTERISTICS

Porcelain plumbing fixtures (bathtubs, toilets and sinks) are designed to stay looking new for years with only a minimum amount of care. To preserve the beauty and gloss of porcelain bathtubs, toilets and sinks, observe one basic rule: NEVER USE ABRASIVE CLEANERS. Abrasive cleaners scratch through glasslike surfaces quickly. Liquid dishwashing detergent on a moist cloth is the preferred method of cleaning.

Although porcelain is durable, take care not to drop heavy articles on it, which might cause chipping. Should chipping occur, porcelain repair services are available. Contact you Builder's Customer Service Department if you have questions about this.

Since water is being used in these fixtures, it is important the joints between the fixtures and the surrounding waterproof surfaces remain sealed. If the seal is not maintained and water is allowed to seep into the joint, there is a possibility of damage to the underlying structure or other component of the home, and it also creates an environment for mold to grow.

MAINTENANCE GUIDELINES

1. Avoid abrasive cleaners and solvents which may ruin porcelain and plastic parts. Clean with a soft, damp cloth and dishwashing detergent, followed by brisk polishing with a clean, dry cloth.
2. Check the joint between the porcelain fixture and the supporting surface periodically for gaps or separation. Use a silicone-based caulk to seal the gaps as needed.

PLUMBING – TUB & SHOWER

MATERIAL CHARACTERISTICS

The tub installed in your home is going to be either a fiberglass tub or a steel tub with a porcelain finish. Both types of tubs will provide years of service if properly maintained.

Fiberglass tubs have a gel coat surface which can crack or scratch if used improperly. However, if damage occurs there are professional re-finishers to be found online, or in your local Yellow Pages which can repair or re-finish the tub to appear as new. Over a long period of time the gel coat may become thin and wear through to the fiberglass, however this is easily remedied by having the tub refinished in place. Also, water in certain regional areas, if not wiped up after bathing/showering, may cause fading or staining of the tub/shower color coat.

Steel tubs have a porcelain finish which is susceptible to scratches or chips if used improperly. There are professional refinishers which can repair or refinish the tub in the event some damage should occur. If combined with a shower installation, the shower surround will typically be installed using ceramic tile.

For the stand-alone shower (without a tub), it may have been installed using a fiberglass stall, or by combining a fiberglass pan or tile pan with a tile surround. The fiberglass shower will have the same material characteristics as the tub.

Maintain your bath and shower areas regularly to prevent mold and mildew build-up and water leakage into the wall spaces. Water which escapes the tub/shower after bathing should be wiped up immediately. The tub/shower area should also be well ventilated during and between uses to allow moisture to dry completely.

MAINTENANCE GUIDELINES

1. Keep the room ventilated by opening doors and windows for cross ventilation when the room is not in use and after use of the tub and/or shower.
2. If your tub/shower is fiberglass, use only a mild, non-abrasive liquid detergent solution to clean it. If water scale has been allowed to build up, attempt to clean it only using a natural product, do not

use chemicals which may dull and/or etch the finish surface. There are special bathroom cleaners available which are specifically formulated for use on fiberglass tubs and showers.
3. You can protect and restore the gloss by applying an acrylic polish or automotive paste wax. Minor scratches can be buffed out using an automotive polishing compound and then following up with a coat of wax. Deep scratches, should they occur, will require professional restoration.
4. Inspect the joint(s) where the fiberglass tub/shower joins the drywall periodically and touch up any shrinkage or gaps in the caulking as needed. Remove and replace any caulking which is showing signs of mildew.
5. Inspect the shower head arm where it penetrates the wall by sliding the escutcheon down and looking for gaps or shrinkage in the caulking. Also check the escutcheons around the valve control(s) to ensure there are no gaps in the caulking. Re-caulk or grout as necessary.
6. To help keep your tile shower and bathtub enclosure walls mildew-free, clean them regularly with a tile cleaner. And frequently use a mold/mildew remover such as chlorine bleach and water solution (1 part bleach to 4 parts water). Be careful not to mix products which are not compatible such as ammonia and bleach.
7. Inspect the joint at the tub to tile location periodically. Touchup shrinkage and gaps by cleaning and filling the dry joint with a flexible caulking compound such as silicone rubber, according to the manufacturer's directions.
8. If you use a rubber or plastic "anti-skid" mat, make sure to remove it from the tub or shower after use to avoid harm to the surface finish.

PLUMBING – WASTE LINES

MATERIAL CHARACTERISTICS

It is normal to hear wastewater from toilets, showers and sinks as it passes through the pipes which are within the walls. It will be more noticeable in a two-story vs. a single-story home.

All of the waste lines in your home are tested before delivery of the home. It is a very rare occurrence for construction debris to be found as the cause for waste line stoppage. If a stoppage does occur, make certain the water supply to the fixture is turned OFF so as to avoid overflow. Contact a qualified service contractor.

There is a common occurrence which can result in a sewer odor at a sink. Each sink has a P-trap in the waste line underneath it to keep sewer gas from backing up into the home. A seal on the line is maintained by a certain amount of water always remaining in the P-trap. If a sink is left unused for a long period of time, the water in the line may evaporate and thus will allow sewer gas to escape up through the drain in the sink. If this does occur, simply run water back into the drain and by doing so the odor should disappear.

MAINTENANCE GUIDELINES

1. Due to mandatory water conservation measures, new toilets use less water than those found in older homes, which reduces the flushing power. To avoid stoppages, it is important to avoid flushing any paper products (including Kleenex tissues, paper towels or feminine hygiene products) other than toilet paper.
2. Grease build-up is the most frequent cause of waste line stoppage; it is recommended to put cooking oils and grease in the household trash. If you must pour these down the drain, always run cold water at the same time. Warm water will cause the oil/grease to coat and eventually clog the pipes.
3. Petroleum-based products, such as paint or lacquer thinner, can damage pipes and should never be poured down the drain.
4. Sink and tub stoppers designed to trap hair and foreign matter should be cleaned regularly to ensure good drainage.
5. Drain cleaning products (such as Drano or Liquid Plumber) can harm waste lines and their use should be avoided.

Important Notice: The waste line clean-out locations should have been identified during your New Home Orientation. In the event your sewer line (from outside of the house to the main in the streets) needs to be professionally cleaned out, care must be taken to ensure the back flow prevention gate valve (if installed) is not damaged in the process. Be sure your contractor is aware of the valve's location. Damage to the gate valve could cause your raw sewage to flow back around your home and onto your property.

PLUMBING – WATER SYSTEM

MATERIAL CHARACTERISTICS

In areas where allowed by the local Building Authority, a type of "high-tech" plastic water pipe may have been used in your plumbing system. This material has been found to be very reliable and it has several advantages. Some of the advantages are: reduction of the number of pipe joints, no soldered joints, reduction of water hammering or pipe groans in the system, flexibility in the system to withstand house movement during settling, earthquake, etc. Plastic pipe is also not susceptible to reaction with common salts or chemicals in the water supply, and the overall life expectancy is greater than most metal pipes.

If the water system in your home has been completed with conventional copper tubing, there are certain material characteristics to be aware of. Hot water passing through the pipe causes expansion and cold water causes contraction. While measures are taken during construction to secure the pipe system to the frame of the house in order to minimize noise caused by expansion and contraction, it is normal to hear some slight sounds in the water system. Because the copper piping is rigid, there may be some slight vibration or groan sounds when the water is turned ON or OFF.

Regardless of the type of water system installed, even though the system has been flushed out to remove dirt or other foreign matter, a small amount of pipe sealant compound may come out of the faucets for the first few days of regular use. This condition is normal with the new plumbing system and should correct itself quickly as the system is being used.

Located at your main supply valve, your water system is equipped with a pressure regulator. The regulator will be set with the appropriate pressure at the time of installation. This device will protect your water system pipes and fixtures from pressure surges in the main water supply distribution lines. Your Builder makes no representations or warranties that the current water pressure level will remain unchanged in the future.

Increasing the water pressure in your home can cause premature wear and tear on pipe joints and faucets and possibly water leaks. If future adjustments are necessary, call a licensed plumber with the capability to measure the pressure and make the adjustment for you.

Your water system has several shutoff points which should be demonstrated to you at the time of your New Home Orientation. Shut off valves are located underneath all sinks, behind the toilets, at the icemaker supply, at the hot water heater and at the washing machine locations. The shutoff for the dishwasher will be located underneath the kitchen sink and may be incorporated with the supply feed to the sink. The stop valves work like a common hose bib. Turning the valve to the right (clockwise) will close the valve. Turning the valve back to the left (counter clockwise) will open the valve. If your water system is the "high-tech" plastic type, a valve lever (as opposed to a round handle) may be located in a recessed box. When the lever is perpendicular to the supply line, the water valve is turned off. Turning the level 90 degrees, parallel with the supply line, will turn the water on.

In the event of a leaky faucet, overflowing sink or an overflowing toilet, the household members must be familiar with the use of these supply valves to be able to shut off the water quickly in order to avoid extensive water damage to the home.

If a water leak is occurring in the system which cannot be controlled by a stop valve, there is a main supply valve which controls water flow to the entire house. This valve is located typically towards the front of the house, or near the garage. You will be able to recognize this is the same location for the pressure regulator, and this may also be the location for the hose-bib servicing the front yard and/or driveway (as identified at your New Home Orientation). Turn the handle clockwise to turn off the water. If a lever controls this valve, when the lever is positioned parallel to the pipe which the valve is mounted on, the valve is open. If the water to the house needs to be turned off, turn the lever so it is perpendicular to the water pipe. Make sure all members of the household are very familiar with the main supply valve location and its operation. Be sure the main supply valve access is not blocked or obscured by landscaping.

A master shutoff valve is located at the water meter. If the water leak is in the yard between the main supply valve to the house and the water meter, or if the main supply valve has failed then shut off the water at the meter. There will be a lock valve positioned at the service pipe running to the house. Typically the top of the valve will have a directional arrow stamped into the surface. If the arrow is running parallel to the service pipe, the valve is open. If the water meter needs to be turned off, turn the valve so it is perpendicular to the water pipe.

If you are unsure about the operation of the water system shutoff(s), please contact you Builder's Customer Service Department and the shutoff(s) will be demonstrated to you. A water system problem carries significant potential for causing damage to the home.

MAINTENANCE GUIDELINES

1. When first moving in, it is advisable to remove all faucet aerators and let all faucets on the system run for about 10 minutes. This will help clear out any residual pipe sealant or other contaminants which may remain in the system.
2. Inspect under each sink in the home frequently to look for possible water leaks at water supply valves. Notify your Builder's Customer Service Department and contact a professional plumber immediately if any leaks are observed.
3. For all shutoff valves other than the water meter, turn the valve all the way to the closed position at least once every six (6) months to insure the valve is able to function properly.
4. If shutting off the water supply at the main, it is advisable when turning the system back on to open a few faucets (sinks and/or tubs) to allow for evacuation of air which may have entered the system during repair work.
5. Review valve shutoff procedures with all home occupants.

ROOF AND GUTTERS

MATERIAL CHARACTERISTICS

The roof and gutter system protects your home from unwanted intrusion of rainwater. Maintaining roof components, especially flashing and roof penetration caulking, is important for prolonging roof integrity.

The gutter and downspout installed on your home has a factory baked paint finish which will require little, if any maintenance for many years.

Roofing materials are quite durable, however, they are not designed to be walked on nor will they support additional weight from decorations, antennas (dishes), solar panels, etc. Over time, as roofing materials are exposed to the elements, they will begin to weather and fade.

Plumbing vent pipes and other roof protrusions are flashed with a sheet-metal collar. The pipe is sealed at the collar with roofing mastic. This mastic expands with heat and contracts with cold, a condition which over time can cause the seal to crack and break.

Periods of strong wind can damage roofing, particularly if the wind exceeds the design specifications for the roof and roofing materials. Such winds can damage roof materials and other components of your home. This type of damage is typically excluded from warranty coverage by the roofing installer and/or manufacturer.

MAINTENANCE GUIDELINES

1. Inspect the roof annually for broken or missing roofing materials. Check again after high winds or driven rains. Have any damaged or missing roofing materials replaced immediately.
2. Visually inspect metal flashing and caulking for separation from chimneys, skylights, roof penetrations and any other construction joints. This may require a ladder carefully and safely placed so as to avoid injury to the inspector or damage to the roof, rain gutters, or landscape. Do not walk on your roof to accomplish this inspection. Use roofing mastic as needed to form a watertight seal at any openings.
3. Remove all accumulations of leaves, plant material and debris from the roof surface, valleys, joints, gutters and flashing areas. Be sure trees growing near the roofline are trimmed back, away from the roof.
4. Keep the roof and gutters free of leaves, plant material, and debris accumulations. Clear the gutters and downspout openings so they are free flowing, and flush out the downspouts so they are running freely.
5. A professional should inspect the roof every few years, with touchup sealing and remedial work completed to prevent possible leaks.

Note: Walking on roofing materials can cause serious damage to the roof covering and possibly breach the roof's integrity. It is highly recommended that you hire a competent and properly licensed professional who will be responsible, and take the necessary care and precautions to perform all inspections, repairs and cleaning.

SHOWER ENCLOSURE

MATERIAL CHARACTERISTICS

There are two (2) different styles of shower doors, either of which may be installed in your home. Bypass sliders operate similar to wardrobe doors. Other shower doors are hinged and operate much like any other standard door found in your home.

The door systems are designed with flanges and/or gaskets which are designed to keep most but not all of the water from the shower from escaping the enclosure. On bypass door enclosures make certain the doors are aligned properly. When standing in the shower the overlapping door (from the inside) should be closest to the showerhead.

It is important to note the shower enclosure does not waterproof the shower from the rest of the room. It is likely some water is going to escape. You can help alleviate some of this problem by pointing the showerhead away from the enclosure as much as possible. After each shower it is important to wipe up any water which may have escaped from the enclosure, as well as monitoring to make certain all adjacent surfaces are drying completely between showers in order to avoid mold or mildew. Clean glass enclosures frequently in order to avoid buildup of water spots.

MAINTENANCE GUIDELINES

1. Allow for proper ventilation.
2. You will be able to maintain the shower enclosure appearance for years with periodic cleaning. Use a mild soap and water to clean the metal frames. Do not use abrasive cleaners or scouring pads.
3. Clean window glass with a sponge and water or a commercial window cleaner.
4. Check the silicone seal around the sides and sill of the enclosure to insure the seal is intact. Touchup with a clear silicone sealant as needed. Avoid sealing drain holes in the shower enclosure as they are intended to allow water to run-off and escape the track.

SHOWER WALLS – CERAMIC TILE

MATERIAL CHARACTERISTICS

See the section titled **COUNTERTOPS – CERAMIC TILE** for the material characteristics of your ceramic tile shower walls.

MAINTENANCE GUIDELINES

1. Allow for proper ventilation.
2. For the other maintenance guidelines see the section titled COUTERTOPS – CERAMIC TILE.
3. Inspect the top of the ceramic tile shower surround for gaps or shrinkage in the caulking between the tile and drywall surface. Re-caulk or grout as necessary. Also look to see water is not allowed to pool in a pocket or depression in the caulk or grout, which can be a location for mold growth. Fill the depression with caulk or grout until the surface is sloped toward the face of the tile surround.
4. Inspect the shower head arm where it penetrates the wall by sliding the escutcheon down and looking for gaps or shrinkage in the caulking. Also check the escutcheons around the valve control(s) to ensure there are no gaps in the caulking. Re-caulk or grout as necessary.

SMOKE DETECTORS

MATERIAL CHARACTERISTICS

A 110- volt smoke detector system with a battery backup is on every floor, in each bedroom, and in each hall which adjoins a bedroom. These installations fully comply with all building code and dire safety requirements.

The smoke alarms are powered by the electrical system. A 9-volt battery in each detector is your backup power source if there is an electrical power failure. When the battery is low, you will hear an intermittent beeping or chirping. Replace the battery as necessary; do not simply remove the battery to keep it from chirping, as this will leave your smoke detector non-functional in the event of a power failure.

The push-to-test button accurately tests all smoke alarm functions. Do not use any other test method. Since this is a safety device, the smoke alarm should be tested weekly to ensure proper orientation.

The smoke detector alarm horn is loud in order to alert individuals of a potential danger. However, there may be limiting circumstances where a household member may not hear the alarm (i.e. the hard of hearing, etc.) If you suspect your smoke alarms may not alert a household member, install and maintain specialty smoke alarms.

Typical smoke alarms can only sound their alarms when they detect smoke. Smoke alarms detect combustion particles in the air. They do not sense heat, flame, or gas. This smoke alarm is designed to give audible warning of a developing fire. Smoke may or may not reach the smoke alarm quickly enough to ensure safe escape.

Smoke alarms have limitations. The smoke alarm is not foolproof and is not warranted to protect lives or property from fire. Smoke alarms are not a substitute for fire insurance. Additionally, it is possible for the smoke alarm to fail at any time, for any reason. For this reason, you must test the smoke alarm often and replace the alarm every ten (10) years. Smoke alarms may be triggered by cooking (i.e. by smoke or steam). Familiarize yourself with the proper method to turn-off the smoke alarm when it is clear that there is no danger.

PRATICE FIRE SAFETY! If the smoke alarm sounds and you have not pushed the test button, it is warning of a dangerous situation. Your immediate response is necessary. To prepare for such occurrences, develop family escape plans and consult the local fire department for tips on safety, and discuss them with your household occupants.

MAINTENANCE GUIDELINES

1. The push-to-test button accurately tests all functions. Do not use an open flame to test the smoke alarm as you may ignite and damage the smoke alarm and/or the home.
2. Each smoke alarm unit should be tested often, at least monthly, and upon returning from vacation or when no one has been in the household for an extended period of time.
3. Test all smoke alarms weekly by doing the following:
    a. Observe the green LED. A constant green light indicates the smoke alarm is receiving 120V AC power.

       b. Firmly depress the push-to-test button for several seconds. The smoke alarm will sound a loud beep about four (4) times per second. The alarm may sounds for up to ten (10) seconds after releasing the push-to-test button.
       c. If smoke alarm does not sound, turn off power at main fuse box or circuit breaker and check wiring. Retest the smoke alarm.
4. Replace the backup battery at least once per year. Replace the existing battery with a similar, new, 9-volt battery. Do not use rechargeable batteries. The battery can be replaced as follows:
       a. Turn off power to smoke alarm at main service panel.
       b. Turn the smoke alarm counter-clockwise to detach from mounting plate.
       c. Gently pull down smoke alarm. Be careful not to separate wire connections.
       d. Pull out power plug from back of smoke alarm.
       e. From back of smoke alarm, lift tab to open battery pocket door.
       f. Remove battery from pocket. Disconnect and discard old battery from battery connector.
       g. Connect a new 9-volt battery to connector. The battery will fit only one way. Be sure battery connector is securely attached to battery terminals.
       h. Place battery into battery pocket.
       i. Close battery pocket door. Push down until it snaps into place.
       j. Replace connector plug. Connector will "snap" into place. Gently tug connector to be sure it is attached properly.
       k. Reattach smoke alarm to mounting plate by turning smoke alarm clockwise until it snaps into plate.
       l. Turn on power and test smoke alarm using push-to-test button
5. Using the soft brush attachment to a vacuum cleaner, vacuum all sides and cover of the smoke alarm often and at least monthly to remove dust, dirt or debris. Do not attempt to clean inside the smoke alarm, as this will void the warranty.

STUCCO

MATERIAL CHARACTERISTICS

Exterior stucco consists of a base coat ("scratch coat" and "brown coat") of cement plaster and a finish coat (or "color coat") of prepared, factory mixed plaster material known as "stucco." Aside from its aesthetic purpose of finishing off the home, stucco's most important duty is to protect the interior of the house form the elements. The building paper below the stucco is what keeps the elements of weather from penetrating to the inside of the home.

Stucco is one of the most durable and low maintenance exterior finishes available. However, over time the original color coat will fade and/or discolor due to sun and weather exposure. Most typically, the dark stucco colors will fade and lighten over time. It is because of these expected material characteristics that if stucco patching or repair is necessary, it is impossible to obtain a perfect match between the original color coat and the repair area.

Cracks in the stucco may form on the surface due to heat conditions during or after application; the drying out process, normal settlement, or natural shrinkage takes place as the stucco matures. Stucco cracking is a normal occurrence and cannot be completely prevented.

Also due to shrinkage of the stucco as it matures, a gap may appear between the stucco and the exterior door frames, window frames, metal vents and/or wood trim. This is a common occurrence; it is not a defect and is considered to be part of Homeowner maintenance. The gap can be filled with a silicone caulking available at any home improvement center.

Certain exterior design features are created from shaped foam that is applied over the stucco "brown coat" and covered with the stucco "color coat". The foam allows for exterior architectural decorations that do not penetrate the water-resistant barrier, as foam is softer than wood. Ladders or heavy objects may damage it. A commercial stucco product, painted or fogged to blend the color can repair nicks or dents in foam and stucco coating.

Stucco wall surfaces should not be penetrated with fasteners or be used as a support surface for other construction (i.e. patio overhead structures, basketball backboards, awnings, etc.). Any integrity violations of the stucco surface could cause water intrusion problems in the future.

One of the most important components of the stucco system is the weep screed. The weep screed is a galvanized metal strip placed at the bottom of the wall. Since stucco is porous, water will penetrate the surface. When the water accumulates it will run down the building paper behind the stucco to the bottom of the wall. The water will escape through the openings of the weep screed. **It is extremely important not to cover the weep screed with any material, or objects which will inhibit this designed flow of moisture.** Specifically, concrete patios, walkways, bricks, planters, soil, etc. should not be installed above the weep screed. It is best to leave at least 2" between the weep screed and these surfaces to allow for proper drainage. If moisture is not allowed to escape through the weep screed, it is likely that moisture will instead backup and flow under the framing plate into the interior of the home. If this occurs, damage may occur with the buckling of wood floors, discoloration of vinyl and ceramic tile grout, and mold growth within walls, under the carpet and pad, or drywall surfaces.

MAINTENANCE GUIDELINES

1. Inspect the joint between window/door/vent frames and the stucco, and apply silicone caulk to close up any gaps which may appear.
2. Adjust irrigation sprinklers to avoid overspray onto the stucco surfaces of the home.
3. Trim plant material away from the home as much as possible as bushes, trees, etc. resting against the stucco surface will be a conduit for moisture.

VENEER – MASONRY

MATERIAL CHARACTERISTICS

Brick or stone is irregular in size and shape and often has small ships and/or surface cracks. This is normal and contributes to the overall texture of the masonry work. The joints between the block/brick are also not perfectly uniform, as the wall is hand laid. Some cracking is normal due to normal ground movement and temperature changes.

Irrigation water may cause a harmless but unsightly condition where a dust of white crystal like material (alkaline) can be seen on the surface of the wall, otherwise known as efflorescence. This is a common occurrence and the removal is part of Homeowner maintenance.

MAINTENANCE GUIDELINES

1. Spraying the affected surface with a mixture of vinegar and water (one part vinegar, four parts water) with a garden sprayer can usually control efflorescence. Heavy buildup may require scrubbing with a stiff brush and/or the use of a pressure sprayer.
2. Mortar cracks can be repaired with a common mortar mix acquired from any home improvement center.
3. Loose brick or stones should be removed and the old grout chipped away from the surrounding brick/stone. New mortar can then be used to reset the original brick/stone following the grout Manufacturer's instructions.

VENTS

MATERIAL CHARACTERISTICS

Your home has several types of vents designed to circulate air, remove hot air, fumes and moisture from the bathrooms, kitchen and laundry room. Vents equipped with a fan are designed to move a specific air quantity (cubic feet per minute of "cfm") as required by building code. Fans make varying degrees of noise by design.

At a minimum, if there is no ventilation to the outside via an operable window, a bathroom shall be equipped with a fan vent.

The laundry dryer vent may have an in-line assist fan and is meant as an exhaust device for the clothes dryer. It is vitally important to inspect and clean lint from the vent hose and vent on a regular basis in order to avoid damage to the dryer equipment and reduce the hazard of fire potential.

MAINTENANCE GUIDELINES

1. Allow for proper ventilation in bathrooms, kitchens and laundry areas.
2. Bath vent fans are low maintenance and require only occasional cleaning of fan blades and vent cover. The fan motor is self-lubricating. If it becomes necessary to replace the fan the modules snaps out, and back-in easily once the unit has been unplugged

from the electrical source. Replacements are available at home improvement centers.
3. Laundry/dryer vents are used often and therefore require frequent maintenance.
    a. Periodically inspect the exterior dryer vent outlet to insure the vent is clear of any lint debris. Do not allow vegetation to grow against or inside of the vent.
    b. Check the interior connection point of the vent to make certain lint has not built up, and make sure the flex hose from the dryer to the vent connection is not crimped or clogged.
    c. Clean out the vent line every six (6) months or as often as needed to keep clear and operational. An obstructed vent line creates a fire hazard and could cause the dryer-heating element to malfunction or burn out.
    d. Inspect the vent flapper at the exterior outlet to insure it opens and closes freely and is not obstructed in any way.
4. On the stove top hood fan which may be located under the microwave oven, remove and clean the grease filter once (1) a month according to the Manufacturers' guidelines. To clean the filter, soak it in a solution of detergent and hot water. Do not use ammonia or ammonia products. Light brushing may be used to remove embedded dirt.

WINDOWS, SLIDING DOORS AND SCREENS

MATERIAL CHARACTERISTICS

The frame of your window may be made from a formed die pattern of solid vinyl with thermally welded corners, which is the most technically advanced product available for new residential homes. Vinyl frame windows are very low maintenance.

The windows and sliding glass doors installed in your home are a consumer product and are guaranteed directly by a Manufacturers' warranty. There is no need to register the warranty to make it effective. This warranty does not apply if the windows and/or sliding glass doors are misused, altered or used for any purpose other than normal household use.

The window and patio door frames and glass typically have some flex, which is normal. The frames may also change shape slightly (bow in or out) with the varying exposure to hot and cold temperatures. Because of these material characteristics there are some operating procedures to keep in mind when opening or closing windows or patio doors. When opening and closing the window, you should move the window in the track by holding the window frame on both sides (using both hands). This will help prevent the window frame from separating from the glass. Opening the patio door does not typically require this same procedure and can be done single handedly unless the frame is sticking due to changing shape. When closing the patio slider it may be necessary to lightly push away or pull the frame towards you in order to have the door align tightly with the vertical track.

Windows are designed to a criterion whereby conditions which exceed the design load (i.e. Heavy driving rains, high winds, etc.) may result in water leaks, which is normal. Therefore, a leak may not indicate a defective window, but one subjected to loads which exceed design criteria.

The weepholes in the bottom of the window track are designed for the removal of excess water. The weepholes are not designed to handle the volume or pressure of water created by a garden hose or by wind driven rains. It is advisable to wash windows by hand to prevent water infiltration.

During cooler weather, air movement near windows may seem like the result of the windows leaking air. This phenomenon is caused when the air outside cools the window glass and the inside air against the glass also starts to cool. The cool air created on the inside will drop to the floor (remember hot air rises) and will thus set a current of cool air in motion.

Most new homes have dual glazed windows in order to meet the energy codes required by your local municipality. A dual glazed window is made of two (2) panes of glass on either side of a frame. This design creates an air space between the glass panes, which is filled with an inert gas to provide insulation. Window tinting may cause excessive heat buildup in this air space, which can result in the failure of the seal and/or the glass cracking. Therefore, applying window tinting will automatically void the Manufacturers" warranty.

A special notice about screens: Window screens and patio door screens are designed solely to keep insects out when your windows are open. They will not prevent humans, even small children, from falling out of a window. Do not allow children to play unsupervised near an open screened window or to place their weight against, or push against a window screen. Even when screened, open windows pose a serious danger to children and furniture should not be placed in a way which gives them easy access to a window.

MAINTENANCE GUIDELINES

1. You will be able to maintain the appearance of the windows for years with periodic cleaning. Use a mild soap and water to clean vinyl frames.
2. Clean window glass with a sponge and water or a commercial window cleaner. The use of hoses to horizontally spray windows is not recommended as the water may enter the home through the weep holes. If this water infiltration does occur, wipe up the water immediately to prevent drywall damage on the interior window sill, etc.
3. Windows in bathroom areas may be subjected to additional moisture on the inside due to condensation from bathing. It is important these windows are cleaned frequently. Special attention should be made to the bottom window track, as this is a place where mold and mildew can grow if not ventilated properly after each bathing use. Spraying this area down with a bleach solution or bathroom cleaner should avoid this problem.
4. There is at least one water weephole in the exterior ledge of the window frame. Be sure weepholes are always open, as water will accumulate if they are plugged. At a minimum inspect the weepholes every six (6) months, before and after the rainy season.
5. If a window sticks or excessive pressure is needed to open or close, apply a silicone spray lubricant.
6. After continuous use, some of the single-hung windows may not stay in place when you open them, sagging slightly. The window tension may require adjustment.
7. Vinyl touchup kits should be available at your local home improvement for repair of minor scratches and blemishes.
8. Window screens are also fragile and should be treated with care. When they are removed for dusting and/or cleaning, use the tabs for careful removal of the screen from the window opening and for careful replacement after cleaning. It is typical for screens to come in, and out, of the window opening in only one direction. Do not force the screen in either direction as this may result in bent or damaged framework. Bent or damaged screens are not covered by the warranty.
9.

YARD DRAINAGE

MATERIAL CHARACTERISTICS

Your lot has been carefully engineered to ensure adequate drainage of rain and irrigation water. All lots have been fine-graded to move water away from the house. Depending upon the design and site condition of your home, yard drains may have been installed to aid in the removal of water. The civil engineer for the project as well as the local Building Dept. has inspected the lot to make certain the final grade is in compliance with code requirements.

It is extremely important you do not alter the drainage slope pattern around your home when installing and maintaining landscaping. Any alteration of or failure to maintain established drainage shall be solely at your risk and solely your responsibility, and shall relieve the Builder of all warranties and liabilities related thereto. It is recommended that you have a licensed civil engineer, landscape architect or other qualified professional approve all landscaping changes to Builder installed drainage to ensure drainage has been properly maintained.

Note: It is vital all planter, yard, sidewalk and patio surfaces slope away from the home in order to prevent water intrusion and the resultant damage it may cause. Additionally, these new hardscape surfaces should also be installed below the weep screed (see the section titled STUCCO for more information).

MAINTENANCE GUIDELINES

1. Visually observe irrigation run-off and make adjustments to the irrigation system or to the finish grade to ensure all run-off is coursing into drainage swales and to the installed drainage devices such as the gutter at the street.
2. **Do not over water** when irrigating your landscaping. Soil may be expansive, which means if it becomes over saturated or conversely becomes too dry the soil will expand and contract. These occurrences can cause movement in the foundation of the home or your landscape improvements, and contribute to cracking, etc.
3. Adjust you irrigation/sprinkler systems(s) frequently to account for climatic and seasonal conditions.
4. Clear any silt build-up monthly which has collected in the drain swales or yard drains which can impair drainage.

5. If installed, flush the yard drain lines monthly to keep them clear of dirt and debris.
6. If drains are prone to clogging, install gravel or small rocks around area drains to help keep the area clear.
7. Re-define the drainage swales, removing any slit or debris which may have collected during prior rains.
8. Repair erosion in drainage swales, as needed, to avoid excessive migration of soil and to maintain positive drainage.
9. Do not allow water to puddle near the foundation of your home.

DESIGN GUIDELINES

When you make landscape and concrete flatwork improvements, please note the following:
1. Building codes do not allow drainage from your property to course onto your neighbor's property. All runoff water from each individual property must course to the public drainage system (storm drain, street, etc.).
2. Do not place permanent planters against the building, as they may cause water to enter your home.
3. Do not change the approved grading.
4. Install additional area drains as needed in patios, walks, or in planted areas to help control water flow.
5. Ensure all installations of patios and walks are installed below the weep screed (as defined in the Section-Stucco), sloped away from the house and the base soils are properly compacted.
6. Do not allow the weep screed to be covered by any type of hardscape, soil or plant material (see the section on Stucco).
7. The condensate drains for your-air conditioning (if installed) must remain clear and in the open to remain functional. Please bring this to the attention of your contractor prior to installation of any material in the area of these drains.
8. Plumbing clean-outs should be left uncovered and unobstructed but they may be shortened if left higher than necessary to permit landscaping in some locations.
9. Hot water pressure relief outlets should be left uncovered and unobstructed.

Note: Before digging, be sure to contact your local utility agency to identify underground utility conduits beneath your property. Once identified, dig with caution, as not all lines may be identified.

BIBLIOGRAPHY AND REFERENCES

American Concrete Institute. (2011). *ACI 318-Building Code Requirements for Structural Concrete.* Farmington Hills, MI.

American Concrete Institute. (2011). *ACI 530- Building Code Requirements for Masonry Structures.* Farmington Hills, MI.

American Forest and Paper Association. (2011) *Wood Frame Construction Manual for One- and Two-Family Dwellings (WFCM).* Leesburg, VA.

American Iron and Steel Institute. (2007). *Standard for Cold-Formed Steel Framing—Prescriptive Method for One - and Two-Family Dwellings (AISI S230).* Washington D.C.

American Society of Heating, Refrigerating and Air-Conditioning Engineers. (2006-2009). *ASHRAE Handbook: Fundamentals.* Atlanta, GA.

Ballast, D. (1994). *Handbook of Construction Tolerances.* McGraw Hill.

Building Industry Association of San Diego County. (1993). *Top 25 Construction Problems and Their Resolution.* Construction Quality Task Force.

California Building Industry Association. (2005). *SB 800, The Homebuilder "FIX IT" Construction Dispute Resolution Law.* Sacramento, CA.

California, State of, Department of Real Estate. (1996). *Operating Cost Manual for Homeowner Association.* Sacramento, CA.

California, State of, Contractor's State License Board. (1982). *Workmanship Guidelines.* Sacramento, CA.

Concrete Committee of San Diego County. (2001). *Concrete Performance Standards and Maintenance guidelines.* San Diego, CA.

Gypsum Association. (2012). *Fire Resistance Design Manual.* Hyattsville, MD.

Hansen, D. & Kardon, R. (2011). *Code Check – Building.* Taunton Press. Newtown, CT.

Hansen, D. & Kardon, R. (2010). *Code Check – Electrical.* Taunton Press. Newtown, CT.

Hansen, D. & Kardon, R. (2011). *Code Check – Plumbing & Mechanical.* Taunton Press. Newtown, CT.

International Code Council. (2007). *California Building Code.* Whittier, CA.

International Code Council. (2007). *California Electrical Code.* Whittier, CA.

International Code Council. (2007). *California Mechanical Code.* Whittier, CA.

International Code Council. (2007). *California Plumbing Code.* Whittier, CA.

International Code Council. (2006-2009). *International Residential Code for One and Two Family Dwellings.* Washington D.C.

International Association of Plumbing & Mechanical Officials. (2009). *Uniform Mechanical Code.* Ontario, CA.

International Association of Plumbing & Mechanical Officials. (2009). *Uniform Plumbing Code.* Ontario, CA.

Journal of Light Construction. (1997). *Troubleshooting Guide to Residential Construction*, Builderburg Group.

NAHM Research Center, Inc. (2001). *Mold in Residential Buildings.* Washington D.C.

National Association of State Contracting Licensing Agencies. (2009). *NASCLA Residential Construction Standards.* Phoenix, AZ.

National Fire Protection Association. (2011). *National Electrical Code.*

National Roofing Contractor's Association. (2007-1009). *NCRA Roofing and Waterproofing Manual.* Vols 1, 2, & 3. Rosemont, IL.

National Wood Flooring Association. (2000). *Problems, Causes and Cures.* Ellisville, MO.

NAHB Home Builder Press. (2005). *Residential Construction Performance Guidelines.* Washington D.C.

New Jersey, State of, Division of Codes and Standards. (2005). *Homeowners booklet*, New Home Warranty Program. NJ.

Reynolds, D. (1998). *Residential & Light Commercial Construction Standards*. R.S. Means, Inc. Kingston, MA.

Sacks, A. (1994). *Residential Water Problems*. NAHM Home Builder Press. Washington, DC.

Structural Building Component Association & Truss Plate Institute. (2006-2013). *Guide to Good Practice for Handling, Installing, Restraining & Bracing of Metal Plate Connected Wood Trusses.*

Tenebaum, D. (1996). *The Complete Idiot's Guide to Trouble Free Home Repair*. Alpha Books. NY.

Truss Plate Institute. (2008). *National Design Standard for Metal Plate Connected Wood Truss Construction*. Alexandria, VA.

ABOUT THE AUTHOR

Ryan Brautovich is an Army veteran with more than 20 years of home construction, home remodeling and building experience who has consulted for Fortune 500 home builders as well as the Top 100 privately held home building companies. He is a custom home builder in California and a California licensed general contractor. Ryan is International Code Council Certified, an International and California Building Inspector as well as an International and California Plumbing Inspector. He is a graduate of Auburn University with degrees in both Accounting and Business Management. He has consulted for the City of Lancaster (CA) Building & Safety Department, K. Hovnanian Homes, Beezer Homes, Pardee Homes, KB Homes, Standard Pacific Homes, American Premiere Homes, Richmond American Homes, DR Horton, and Frontier Homes – just to name a few.

Ryan founded the Construction H.E.L.P. Foundation, a national nonprofit organization, dedicated to advocating for and meeting the needs of individuals who have suffered at the hands of unscrupulous contractors and sub-contractors who simply took advantage of the helpless homeowner in order to make a quick buck – and either didn't finish the project, overcharged or simply took money and didn't perform the work as promised. Over the years, the number of phone calls Ryan received increased dramatically from frustrated and angry homeowners who were desperately seeking help after being ripped off by other contractors. As a result, he founded the Construction H.E.L.P. Foundation, and it's educational assistance program – Home Construction Audit – to provide assistance and education to homeowners. As the founder of the Construction H.E.L.P. Foundation, Ryan has made it the organization's daily mission to return ethics to the home building and home remodeling profession and provide homeowners with the expert help and crucial knowledge they need so that they will never be taken advantage of again.

www.ingramcontent.com/pod-product-compliance
Lightning Source LLC
Chambersburg PA
CBHW021146230426
43667CB00005B/274